Perspective Drawing

The Projected Image Method

Harry Merritt

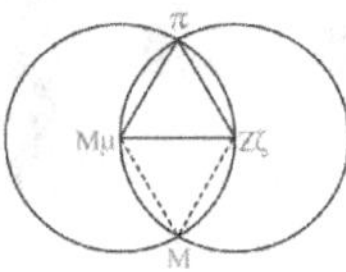

Culicidae
Architectural Press

Ames | Berlin | Gainesville | Tokyo

Second Edition, first published in 2008 by
Culicidae Architectural Press
an imprint of Culicidae Press, LLC
918 5th Street
Ames, IA 50010-5906
USA

www.cularchpress.com

ISBN-13: 978-0-6151-8696-2

Table of Contents

PREFACE

It seems anachronistic to write a book on manual perspective-drawing when freely available computer software can generate impressive three-dimensional views faster than it takes to read these lines. And yet, here it is, a book about a method to draw perspectives by hand.

It might be helpful to take a long yet brief view—the word 'perspective' derives from the Latin *perspicere*, literally 'to see through'—into the history of representing what we see, or imagine, on a flat surface. In a recent New Yorker magazine article about the Chauvet caves, located in the Ardèche region of France, the author Judith Thurman points out that the stone age artists, who painted the interior of the caves, used perspective drawing techniques that would lie dormant for another 35000 years or so until their rediscovery during the Renaissance. Earlier Greek philosophers had developed theories of perspective, but it would take until the early 1400s to have a technique in place that could be used to accurately depict three-dimensional space. Examples such as Brunelleschi's empirical experiments in drawing the St. Giovanni Baptistry next to the Duomo in Florence, Leonardo da Vinci's *Last Supper*—aside from its religious meaning

a precise exercise in one-point perspective—and Albrecht Dürer's oddly erotic woodcuts, such as *Der Zeichner des liegenden Weibes* (from *Underweysung der Messung,* Nürnberg, 1538), represent the rebirth of carefully constructed perspective drawing.

500 years later we have the exquisitely crafted graphite perspectives by Monica Ponce de Leon and Nader Tehrani from Studio dA, Daniel Castor's instructive jellyfish drawings, and Lauretta Vinciarelli's symmetrical and light-filled water color constructions, but the question remains: why create perspectives manually today in the age of digital reproduction? One could answer that there have always been perspective-drawing aficionados who may simply want to add another technique to their tool box, but there are other arguments to consider. One reason to take on a deliberate, manual approach to creating perspectives lies in re-discovering the basic pleasures of drawing by hand. The simple effort it takes to arrange the tools—pencil, ruler, paper, sharpener, eraser—on a table, as well as the preparatory action of laying out the drawing space, stands in sharp and perhaps desirable contrast to pushing a button with a pointing device on a flat screen. Furthermore, the haptic pleasure of sharpening

a pencil, holding it in the hand, and running it along a metal or plastic ruler, hearing the faint sound of the graphite being transferred to the paper, and slowly developing a view of a three-dimensional world on a flat surface is nothing short of magical.

Another argument may be the realization that any kind of manual drawing helps us see *what* we draw—a representation of an existing or projected reality—differently as we go through a process of re-drawing what we see—and *how* we see—in our mind's eye or in front of us. In the case of architectural projects or designs, manual perspective drawing becomes a way to make the imagined spaces visible before a client's eyes, allowing further development of the design without hindering the process by being too explicit. Unlike a digital sketch, a hand-drawn perspective has an openness, a capacity to be altered because it is merely a hand drawing. It's ordinariness is not a liability but an asset. In the case of drawing what we see in front of us, accurate perspectives will allow us to see the world more acutely than a photograph or a digital perspective of the same scene would ever reveal. The constant decision-making process about what to include—and exclude—in a manual drawing helps us become better designers.

Finally I shall add a disclaimer and reveal an ulterior motive for writing the preface to this book: Professor Harry Merritt was a teacher of mine when I was an undergraduate student of architecture at the University of Florida—in the late 1980s—and he taught the method presented here to everyone in his studio, and no doubt to legions of other students during his tenure at Florida. For many years since then he has advanced this drawing method through several iterations, and now this book includes detailed instructions on drawing anything using a one-, two-, or three-point perspective. On the next page an elaborately constructed perspective drawing of mine from 1984—prior to getting into architecture—shows a different and much less elegant method than the one explained in this book. I wish now that I had known the Projected Image method earlier....

As a student I remember Harry's infamous use of gridded paper sheets—he prefers ¼ inch grids—on which he would sketch out perspective views with amazing speed. As young kids bitten by the emerging computer bug—I was using Architrion software by 1989 on Macintosh II machines—we were initially doubtful that this seemingly old-fashioned way to draw would be useful, but we quickly realized the potential and power of using Harry's method to make visible what we imagined.

More important than learning how to draw is to design in three dimensions, i.e. spatially. Most architects, even today, still conceive their designs in two dimensions, and the reason for this behavior may well lie in the preponderance of the plan drawing as a useful but utterly inappropriate means to design three-dimensional space. Harry taught us early on that, as designers and human beings living in space bounded by architecture, we have to inhabit this imagined reality in at least three

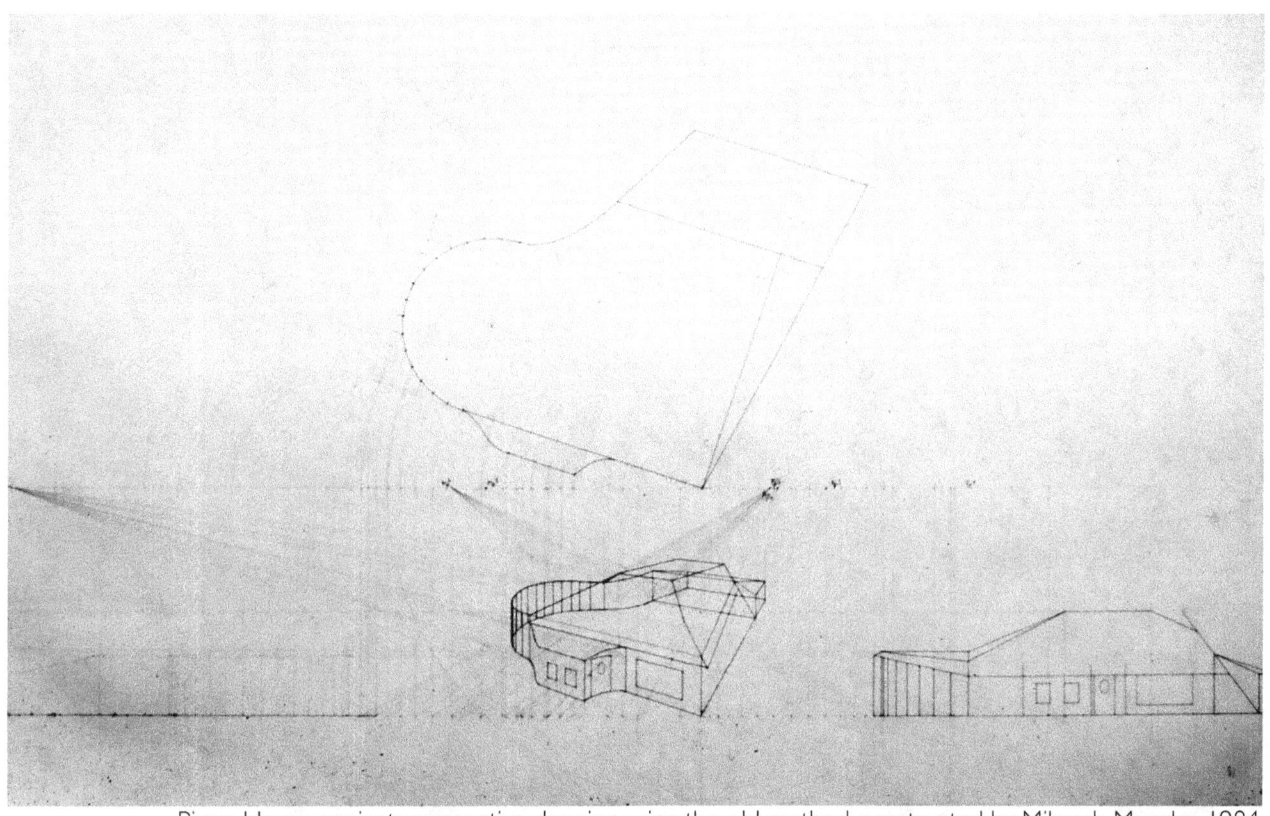

Piano House project; perspective drawing using the old method, constructed by Mikesch Muecke, 1984.

dimensions. Using perspective drawing as a tool is an efficient means to design not only spatially but also to develop crucial visualization skills that aid designers in projecting into the future what the world around us *might* become.

While the pleasure of viewing a completed hand-drawn perspective is instantaneous, it is usually followed by the question: how did they do that? This book provides an answer by teaching the reader how to use Harry Merritt's Projected Image system to draw any three-dimensional space on a piece of paper.

It's a great pleasure to be able to offer Harry's knowledge and wealth of experience in perspective drawing to an expanded audience that will hopefully find as much enjoyment and utility in drawing as Harry and his students have over the years.

Mikesch Muecke
Gainesville, Florida
January 2010

FOREWORD

This book is not about "how to draw." It does not discuss drawing technique, drafting, orthographic or paraline drawing, shades and shadows or many other important elements of drawing that all design students should master.

This book is not about design. It does not discuss the philosophy of the organization of space and form.

There are many excellent books on the above subjects and this book (or manual) is not intended as a substitute or replacement but, possibly, as a supplement.

This book is about perspective and a method to quickly and accurately construct the perspective drawing.

Architecture is about SPACE and the resultant form and structure. The successful designer must develop the ability to think conceptually and to interpret such thoughts into space and form. The inability to draw space and form in perspective is a significant handicap.

The design process involves a sequence of continuous decision-making by the designer. Any serious pause in this process, such as the laborious construction of a perspective to view the spactial decisions made to date, can impair the designer's thought process and break the chain of intellectual events so necessary to a productive design effort.

Architecture is to a large degree a visual art, and a designer cannot work only with orthographic or paraline drawings. The designer can be much more productive if ideas and concepts can be made spatially visible during the design process. Most current methods of manual perspective drawing that are necessary to make space visible are either laborious and time-consuming or based on an element of guesswork. The first stops the chain of design events, and the other creates possible inaccuracies, thus producing unreliable information.

The Projected Image method, presented in this book, is an attempt to bring accuracy to the perspective drawing with the least interruption to the design process.

INTRODUCTION

The perspective is the only drawing that simulates a true image of a three dimensional environment. Orthograpic drawings are helpful in depicting the shapes of objects in plan, section, and elevation, while paraline drawings are useful in understanding the basic geometry of objects. The perspective is the only drawing that can depict space.

The perspective drawing is an important design tool. Unfortunately, in most cases, the perspective is used as a presentation method to present work already designed. While this is a proper use of the perspective drawing, it contributes little to the design process.

It is my belief that the reluctance of most architecture students, and indeed the architectural profession at large, to use the perspective drawing as a design tool can, for the most part, be blamed on the perspective drawing methods taught by many of our schools and universities. An examination of the basic concepts of perspective drawing taught at the beginning of the 20th century differs little from most of the methods used today.

Many might argue that a method that has survived for this length of time must have value, and even though I agree that there is value in the old method, I believe that the old method is not 'user-friendly', and I think a new system is needed.

Some teachers of perspective drawing encourage the use of perspective charts, which force the designer into preordained vanishing points and station point location. This suggests that the designer impose fixed relationships relative to the view and position in the space prior to investigating the space itself. At best, the use of perspective charts points towards presentation, and not design investigation.

The Projected Image system solves many of the old problems inherent in the old methods. The system embodies a rational explanation of the creation of vanishing points, allows the use of any scale for the perspective drawing irrespective of the scale of the plan, and makes it unnecessary to have the vanishing points fall on the drawing surface, if the location of such points is inconvenient to the designer.

A perspective system must be quick and accurate; but, most of all it must be rational. It is my position that if the designer does not understand how a system works that he or she cannot then orchestrate the system to respond to the exact needs of spatial analysis.

Unlike other perspective methods, the Projected Image system uses the same quick procedures to create a three-point perspective as is used to create a two-point perspective. Because of the complexity of the conventional three-point perspective method, the leading textbooks on drawing used by students today either dismiss the three-point perspective as too difficult to construct or ignore the subject altogether. Indeed, it is the rare professional architect who feels competent in the use of the three-point perspective.

The designer should have the freedom to choose the appropriate drawing, whether one-, two- or three-point, to examine and explain the spatial organization of his or her design without great concern for the effort of perspective construction.

I have been told by many students and faculty alike that learning to draw perspectives is a thing of the past and that the computer has replaced the need for such knowledge, and that I am a dinosaur. The computer is indeed an excellent instrument for the development and examination of a design but as a mere machine it is no match for the skilled designer who can construct ten quick accurate perspectives—and abandon nine to get to an informed analysis of an architectural space—in the time it takes to load the data necessary to produce a computer-generated perspective. Indeed I believe that the two can work hand in hand. Once a basic design of a space is purposed using the Projected Image Method, he data can then be loaded into a CAD program which will produce many instant images of the spatial sequence.

The basic concept of the Projected Image perspective system is that images of elements whose size (in perspective) is not known, can be projective on elements whose size is known; thus, being able to make a drawing of the relationship between the two.

The Projected Image system of perspective construction will create quick and accurate perspectives. Misleading others with drawings that do not faithfully depict the design intent is a serious failing. Misleading yourself significantly reduces your potential growth as a designer.

Chapter 1

The Perspective Drawing

Even though the Projected Image system of constructing perspectives differs from the conventional methods of perspective drawing, there is a series of basic elements and concepts that are applicable to all perspective representations.

These basic elements and concepts are well known to designers who have experience in perspective drawing and they may wish to move to the next chapters after a quick review.

I would advise all beginning students to read with care the following concepts as these ideas are essential to the Projected Image Method. I would also advise the experienced designer to review the section on station point location in one-, two-, and three-point perspectives, as the centerline ($\mathcal{C}$) of the vertical and horizontal cone of vision is most important to the Projected Image Method of perspective drawing.

Cone of Vision

The clear perceptible vision of the human eye's cone of vision is about 60°, or 30° to the right and 30° to the left of the center line (₡) of this visual cone. This is true in both the horizontal and vertical mode (see Figures 1 and 2).

Figure 1 shows the constraints of the horizontal cone of vision for all perspective drawings: one-, two-, and three-point. Figure 2 shows the constraints of the vertical cone of vision for the one- and two-point drawing. In a three-point perspective the ₡ of the vertical cone of vision is not constrained by the horizon line, and the viewer is free to look up or down within the 60° cone of vision and place the ₡ of the vertical cone of vision on any point the designer feels appropriate for the examination of form and space. Figure 3 illustrates the vertical cone of vision for all perspective drawing.

Figure 1: Horizontal Cone of Vision

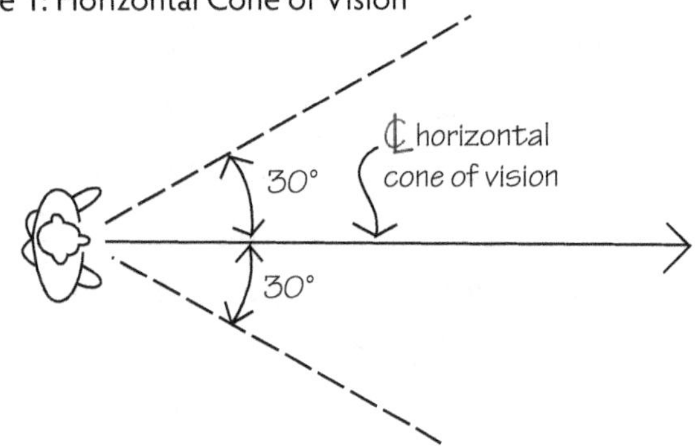

Figure 2: Vertical Cone of Vision

Figure 3: Vertical Cone of Vision

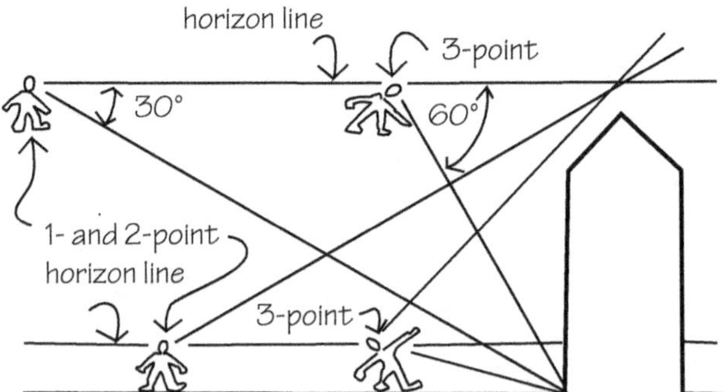

Horizon Line (HL)

On Earth, the horizon line will always be with you as you look straight out. The horizon line is always even with to the viewer's eye. This is true even if flying at 30,000 feet altitude in an airplane.

Station Point (SP)

The Station point is where you are. It is your viewpoint of the object or space to be drawn. Remember, the horizon line will always be at your eye level at your station point.

Ground Plane (GP) and Ground Line (GL)

The ground plane is the horizontal plane from which most vertical measurements in the one-, two-, and three-point perspective are taken.

The ground line is the intersection of the picture plane and the ground plane. This is a very important line in the three-point perspective.

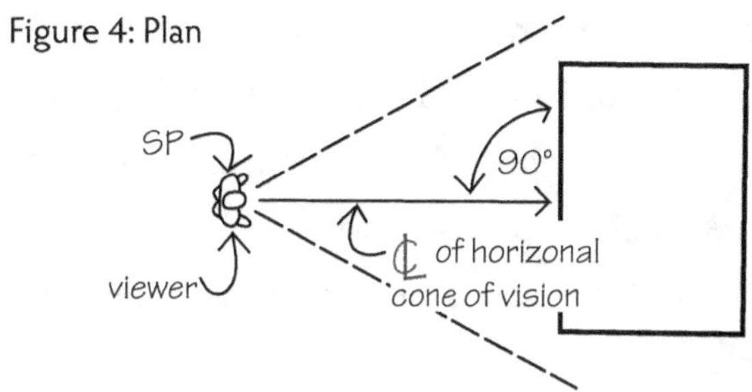

Figure 4: Plan

Figure 5: Section

Types of Perspectives

One-Point Perspective

In a one-point perspective the centerline ℄ of the horizontal cone of vision is parallel or perpendicular to the major planes of the space or object being drawn (Figure 4), and the ℄ of the vertical cone of vision is on the horizon line (HL) (Figure 5).

The one-point perspective is useful in depicting interior spaces and smaller exterior spaces, but it tends to create static views. The location of the ₵ of the cone of vision on the ₵ of the space to be viewed should be avoided as this location creates a "bookmatch" between opposing vertical planes and reinforces the static nature of the one-point perspective drawing.

Two-Point Perspective

The two-point perspective allows the ₵ of the viewer's horizontal cone of vision to be at any angle to the object or space being viewed (except 90°; that's a one-point perspective) that best explains the designer's intent (Figure 6) but the ₵ of the vertical cone of vision must be on the horizon line as in the one-point perspective

(see Figure 5 on previous page).

The two-point perspective drawing is probably the most useful perspective in depicting form and space and comes closer to approximating the geometry of the environment in which we live.

Both the one- and two-point perspectives require that the ₵ of the vertical cone of vision be located exactly on the horizon line and that only the parts of the object or space that fall 30° above or 30° below the horizon can be viewed without distortion.

This is not a serious restriction when viewing our normal environment from the ground plane or viewing the interior of most buildings; however, when tall objects are to be viewed from the ground or objects or spaces are to be viewed from high above, or high interior spaces are to be viewed, the three-point perspective may be the best choice.

Three-Point Perspective

The ₵ of the horizontal cone of vision is not parallel or perpendicular to the major planes of the object or space being viewed and the ₵ of the vertical cone of vision is never on the horizon line (see Figure 7 on

Figure 6

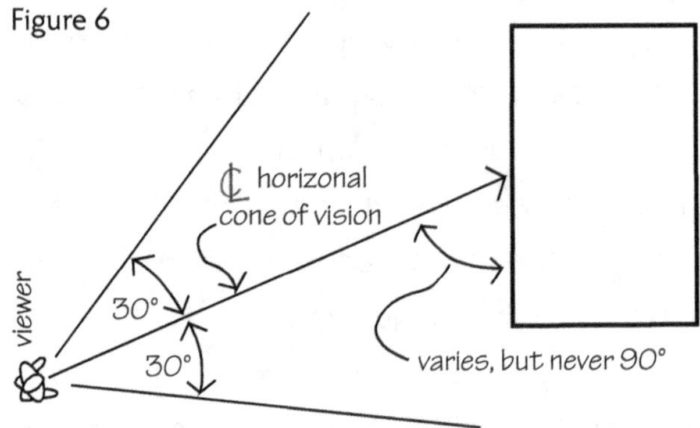

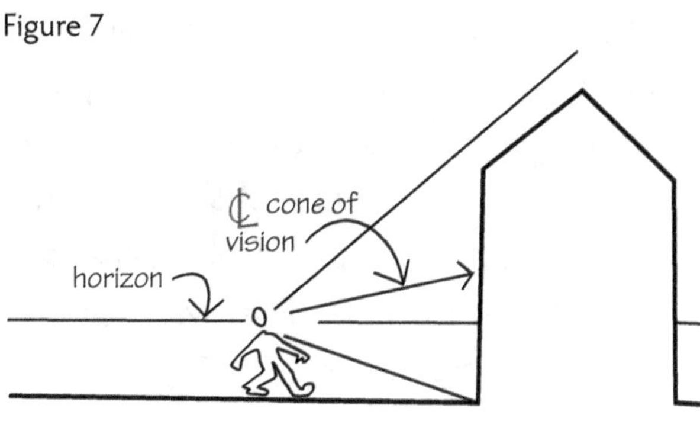

next page). One great advantage of the three-point perspective is the ability of the viewer to cast his or her 60° cone of vision either upward or downward without being constrained by the horizon, as is the case in the one- and two-point perspective. The three-point perspective allows the viewer to move much closer to the object than in the one- or two-point perspective.

Picture Plane (PP)

The most important element in the perspective drawing, and probably the most difficult for designers to visual-ize, is the picture plane. The picture plane is, in reality the surface of your drawing. Indeed, when we draw a perspective, we are really drawing the image of the object on the elevation, the surface, of the picture plane. The picture plane is flat and two-dimensional; the drawing on the surface of the picture plane is also two-dimensional, even though it is an image of a three-dimensional space or object.

Think of the picture plane as a large sheet of glass placed between you and the object or space to be drawn. If you could stand at the station point (from where you view the object) and aim a rifle at the top and bottom of all corners of the object, the bullet holes in the glass would create all the points—when connected by lines—needed to delineate the drawing. This is similar to the way film in a camera records the image of an object as seen by the viewer. The film becomes the picture plane.

Every element of the drawing is located on the picture plane. The horizon line is not back behind the object or space but is on the picture plane. The picture plane is a scorecard on which all elements of the drawing are recorded.

The placement of the picture plane relative to the object being viewed is really the element that determines if a drawing is a one-, two-, or three-point perspec-tive. In a one-point perspective the picture plane is always vertical and is parallel and

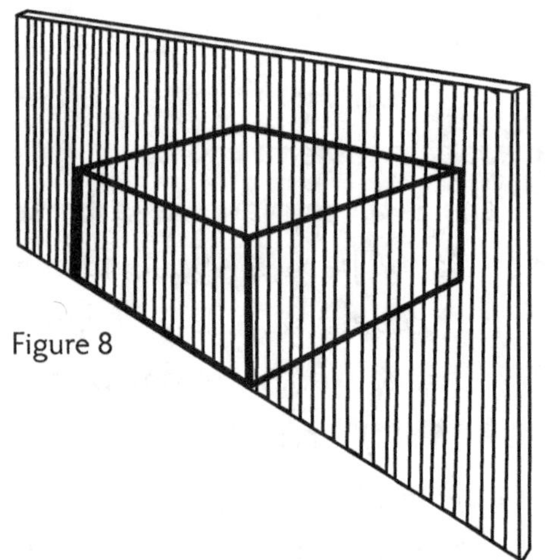

Figure 8

One-Point:
Picture PLane is vertical and parallel or perpindicular to the major planes of the objcet.

Figure 9

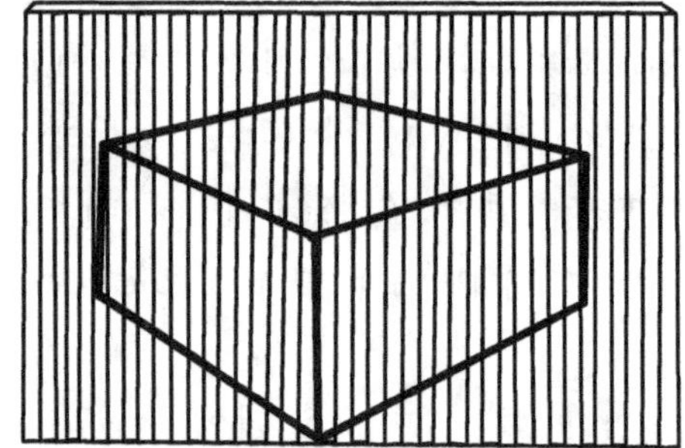

Two-Point:
Picture PLane is vertical and never parallel to the major planes of the object.

Figure 10

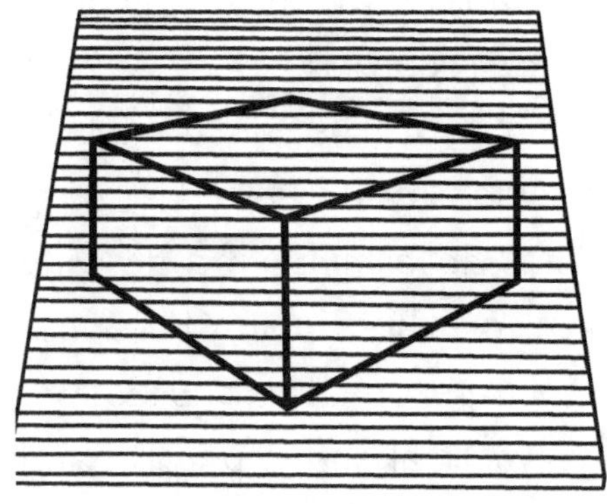

Three-Point:
Picture Plane is never vertical or parallel to the major planes of the object.

perpendicular to the major planes of the object (Figure 8). In a two-point perspective the picture plane is always vertical and never parallel to the object (Figure 9). In a three-point perspective the picture plane is never vertical and never parallel to the object (Figure 10).

Vanishing Points (VP)

All sets of parallel lines that are not parallel to the picture plane appear to converge toward a common point called a vanishing point (VP).

All sets of parallel lines, parallel to the horizon, appear to converge toward a common vanishing point located on the horizon line.

The understanding of the above two principles of perspective allows us another way of defining the one-, two-, and three-point perspective.

In a one-point perspective all lines and planes that are parallel to the picture plane have no vanishing point. Lines and planes that are not parallel to the picture plane vanish to a single point. In Figure 11 (see next page) the front and rear plane are both parallel to the picture

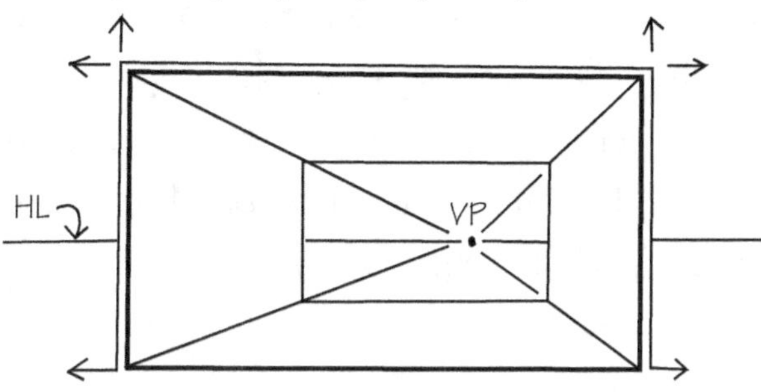

plane and have no vanishing point. The top, bottom, and side planes are not parallel to the picture plane and therefore vanish to a common point.

In a two-point perspective the picture plane is never parallel to the major planes of the space or object; therefore, all lines and planes (not parallel to the picture plane) will vanish toward a common vanishing point, one to the left (VPL) of the $\mathbb{C}$ of the cone of vision and one to the right (VPR) of the $\mathbb{C}$ of the cone of vision. In Figure 12 the front and

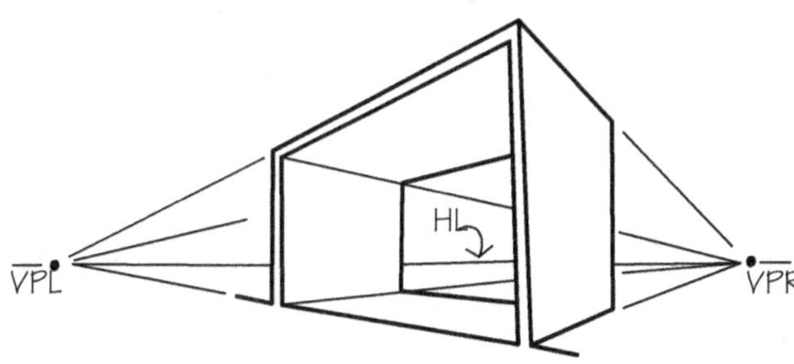

rear planes vanish to the VPL and the side planes vanish to VPR. The top and bottom planes vanish to both VPL and VPR.

In a three-point perspective the picture plane is never parallel to the major horizontal or vertical planes of the space and both the horizontal and vertical planes will have vanishing points.

In Figure 13 the vertical planes vanish to VPL or VPR and to VP3, and the horizontal planes vanish to VPL and VPR. The third vanishing point appears above or below the horizon depending on whether the $\mathbb{C}$ of the vertical cone of vision is being cast upward or downward.

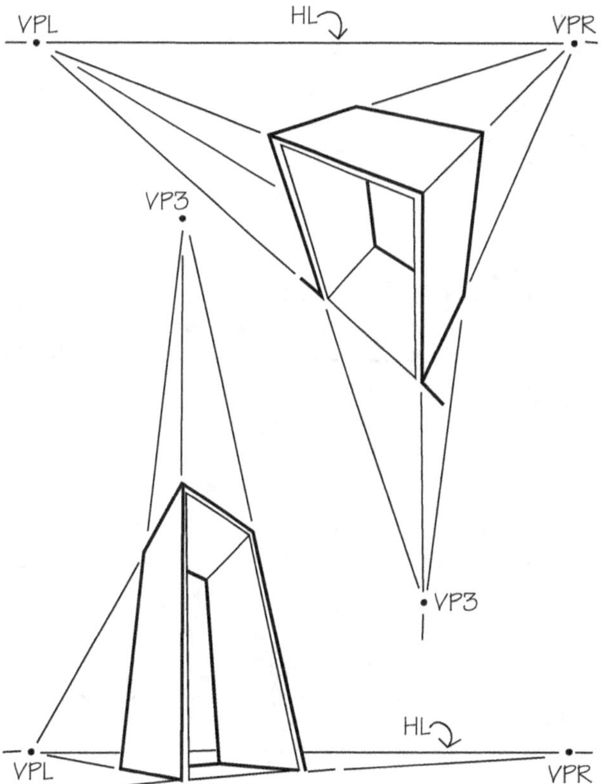

Effects of Position on View

The distance from the viewer (SP) to the object to be drawn has a direct and sometimes dynamic effect on the geometry of the form. The closer the viewer is to an object, the sharper the angles of the form will become (Figure 14). Conversely, the further the viewer is from the object, the flatter the forms will appear (Figure 15).

As the angle of the centerline of the horizontal cone of vision ($\mathcal{C}$ HCV) decreases relative to the plane being viewed, the vanishing point for that plane moves closer to the viewer. Conversely when the angle of the $\mathcal{C}$ HCV increases relative to the plane being viewed the vanishing point for that plane moves further from the viewer (Figure 16).

Figure 16
Angle of View

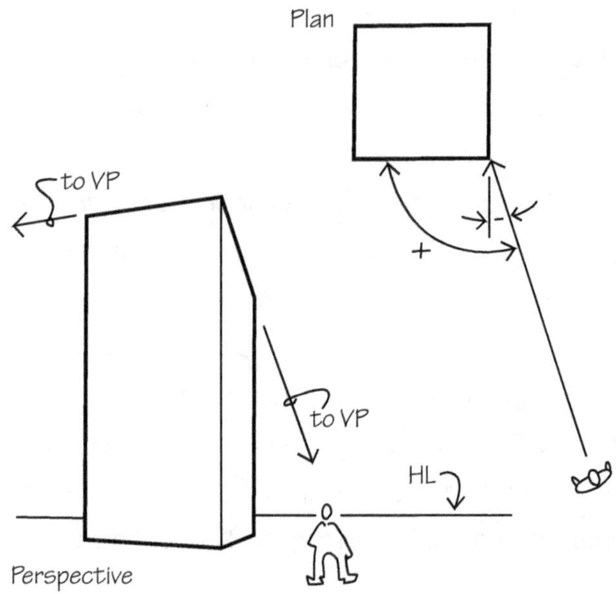

Figure 14
Viewer Close to Object

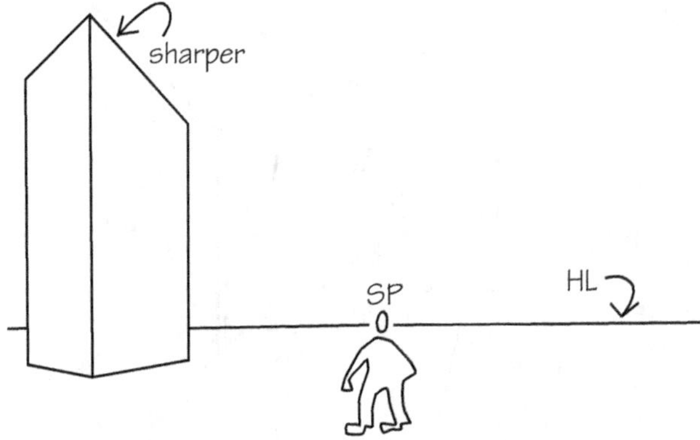

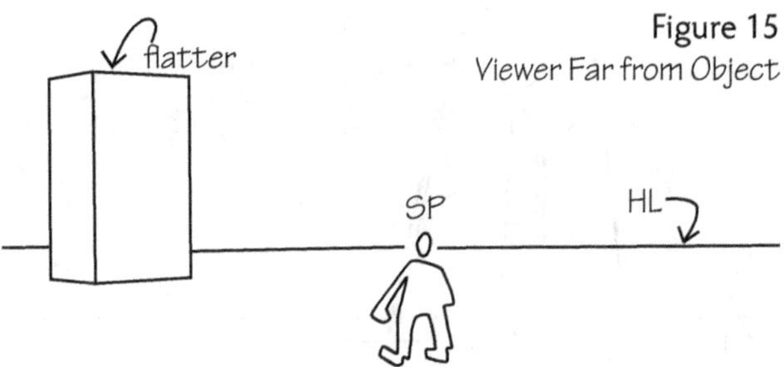

Figure 15
Viewer Far from Object

Height of View

The height above the ground plane from which an object or space is viewed will have a significant effect on the dynamics of the perceived geometry of the form of the object and space.

If an object is viewed from near the ground plane, the top of the object will, depending on its height, create a strong figure-ground relationship with the sky that clearly defines the form of the top of the object above the horizon line and diminishes the contrast of the form relative to the ground plane (Figure 17).

Conversely, if an object is viewed from far above the ground plane, the geometry of the base of the object will be clearly defined relative to the ground plane, and the form of the object near the horizon line will diminish relative to the skyline (Figure 18).

Figure 17
View from Below

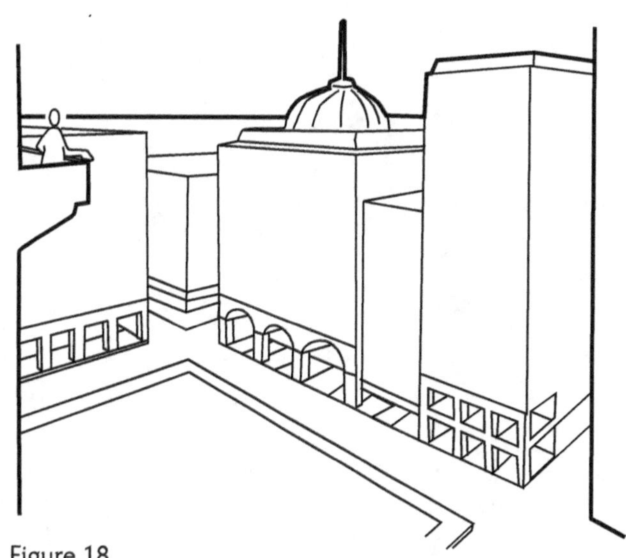

Figure 18
View from Above

CHAPTER 2

The Two-Point Perspective

I have chosen to discuss the two-point perspective prior to an explanation of the one-point, as is normal convention in books on perspective drawing. The two-point perspective most clearly explains the concepts of the Projected Image system. Therefore the one-point perspective is discussed in the next chapter.

The following Projected Image method to construct a two-point perspective contains many of the traditional elements of perspective drawing, but introduces the designer to a new and quick procedure of establishing the form of objects and space in perspective.

The basic concept of the Projected Image system of perspective drawing is the projection of images of elements whose size, in perspective, is not known, on elements whose dimensions are known. We are thus able to measure the relative difference between the two.

Obviously elements of the same size appear smaller as they move further away from the viewer. The Projected Image system of perspective construction is based on a method that enables us to measure this apparent difference.

There is a series of basic steps that will assist in the construction of the perspective. Each step is quick and simple but important to the ultimate accuracy of the perspective.

It is important to remember that the cone of vision is about 60° and any elements falling outside this visual cone will be distorted if you choose to include such elements in your drawing. It is also very important that this 60° cone of vision be divided into two 30° sectors on each side of the ℄ of the cone of vision. This is important as the ℄ of the horizontal cone of vision creates the relationship of the picture plane to the object being drawn, and the ℄ of the vertical cone of vision is the horizon line.

To begin the construction of a two-point perspective, a plan of the object is drawn at a convenient scale and the location from

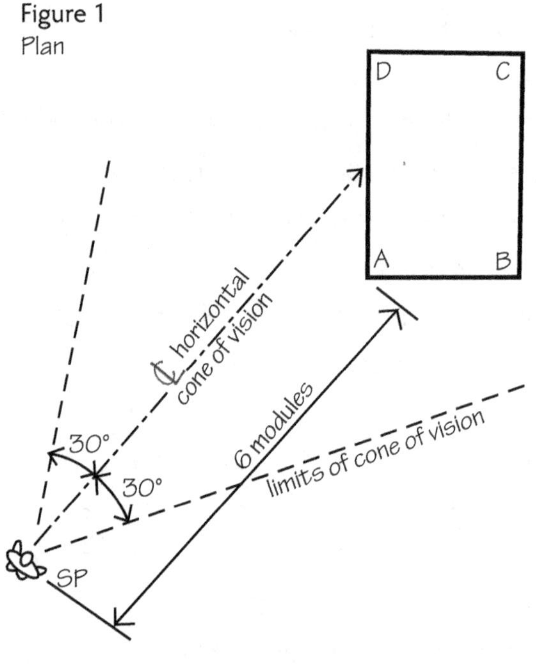

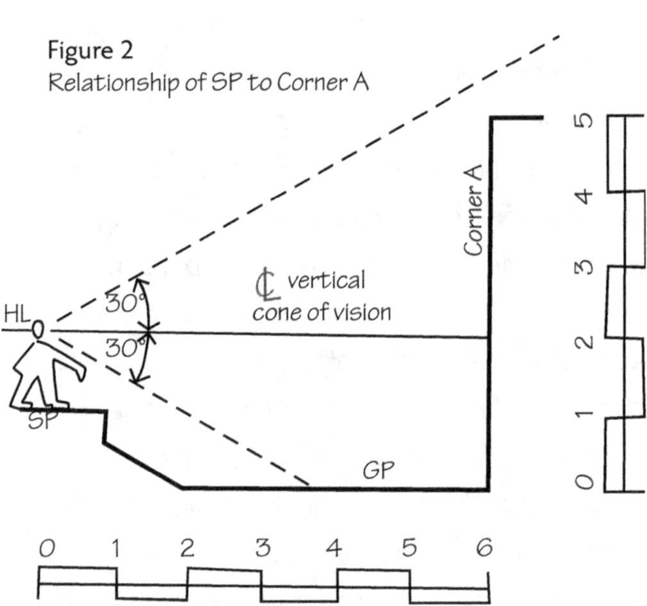

which you wish to view the object is established (SP).

The position of the Station Point is the product of the designer's desire to view the object from a specific point, the constraints placed on this Station Point by the 60° horizontal cone of vision and the 30° sectors of clear vision to each side of the ℄ of this cone, and, the 60° vertical cone of vision. It is quickly apparent, in the adjacent example (Figures 1 and 2) that the vertical cone of vision controlled the placement of the Station Point, as a 30° sector of clear vision cast above the horizon line (Figure 2) is very close to the top clearance in the right and left 30° sectors in the 60° horizontal cone of vision. The height of the SP above the Ground Plane (GP) also affects the distance from SP to the object.

The following examples, using the Station Point as established in Figures 1 and 2, will show the procedure leading to the construction of the two-point perspective drawing.

Lay out the Plan at an appropriate scale, locate the Station Point (SP) and the Picture Plane (PP) as shown in Figure 3.

24

You can use a module of an appropriate scale to measure distances; for example, you can use a foot (12") for buildings of small scale or you can use a module of 5 feet or 10 feet for large-scale buildings.

Remember, the Picture Plane must always be 90° to the ℄ of the horizontal cone of vision. It is helpful, though not mandatory, to pass the Picture Plane through a corner of the object nearest the viewer. This corner (corner A) will become the True Height Line (THL), and all measurements will be taken from this line.

As previously mentioned, you can think of the Picture Plane as a large sheet of glass that has been erected in front of the object to be drawn. As you extend lines from the Station Point to corners A, B, and D, through the Picture Plane, note where these lines cross the Picture Plane (Figure 4). These points have been noted as points Dpp, App and Bpp. These points create line *Dpp-App-Bpp which will become important in the construction of the final perspective.

*pp denotes that these points fall on the Picture Plane (PP).

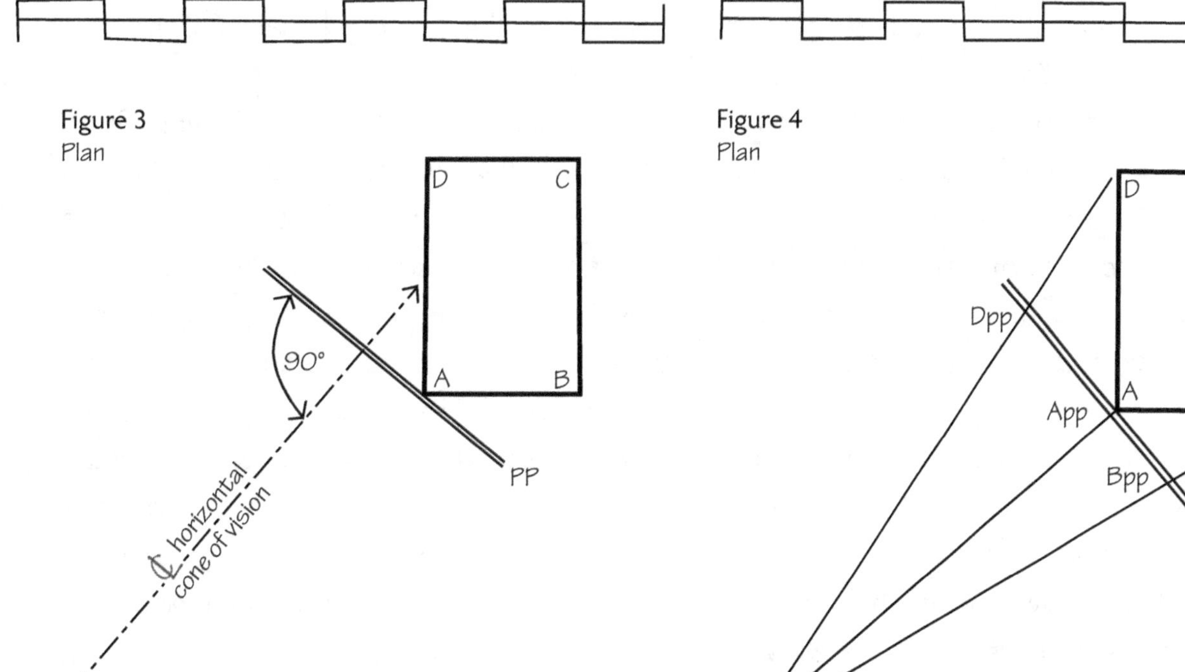

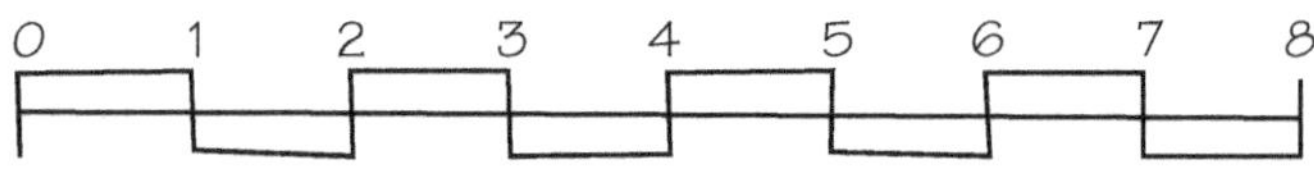

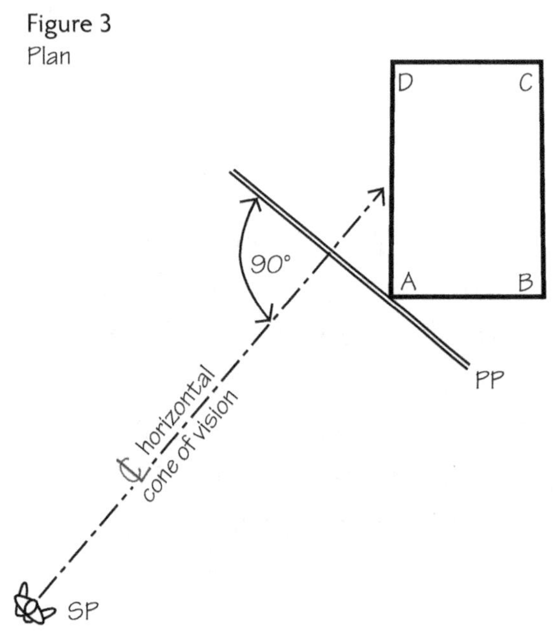

Figure 3
Plan

of vision was 45° to the plane being viewed, the distance from the Center of the drawing to the vanishing point would lessen, and if this angle was reduced to 30°, the vanishing point of the plane being viewed would move still closer to the center of the drawing format.

One of the main advantages of the Projected Image system is that vanishing points that fall off the drawing surface present no problem to the designer as the angle at which a plane vanishes can be found without the use of vanishing points.

You will notice, in Figure 3 (repeated above for ease of reference), that the ℄ of the horizontal cone of vision can be placed anywhere on the object that the designer chooses; however, the selection of this ℄ has a significant effect on the location of the vanishing point of the plane on which this ℄ of vision falls. The greater the angle of the ℄ of the cone of vision to the plane being viewed, the further the vanishing point will move away from the center of the drawing.

In other words, if the ℄ of the cone of vision was at an angle of 80° to the plane being viewed, the vanishing point for this plane would be far away from the center of your drawing and probably off the drawing surface. If the angle of the ℄ of the cone

The Vertical Diagram

The Vertical Diagram is the most important step in the construction of the two-point perspective, and it embodies the basic concept of the Projected Image perspective system.

Imagine that corners A, B, and D, (in Figure 6, bottom right on the next page) are vertical poles and that you could arrange these poles along a single line. You could then look down this line of poles, as you might look down a line of telephone poles, and observe the apparent diminishing height of these poles as they marched toward the horizon (Figure 5 clarifies this in a perspective drawing). If you could measure the height of the pole nearest you (the true height pole) and look at all the other poles through this pole, you could then mark the apparent height of

26

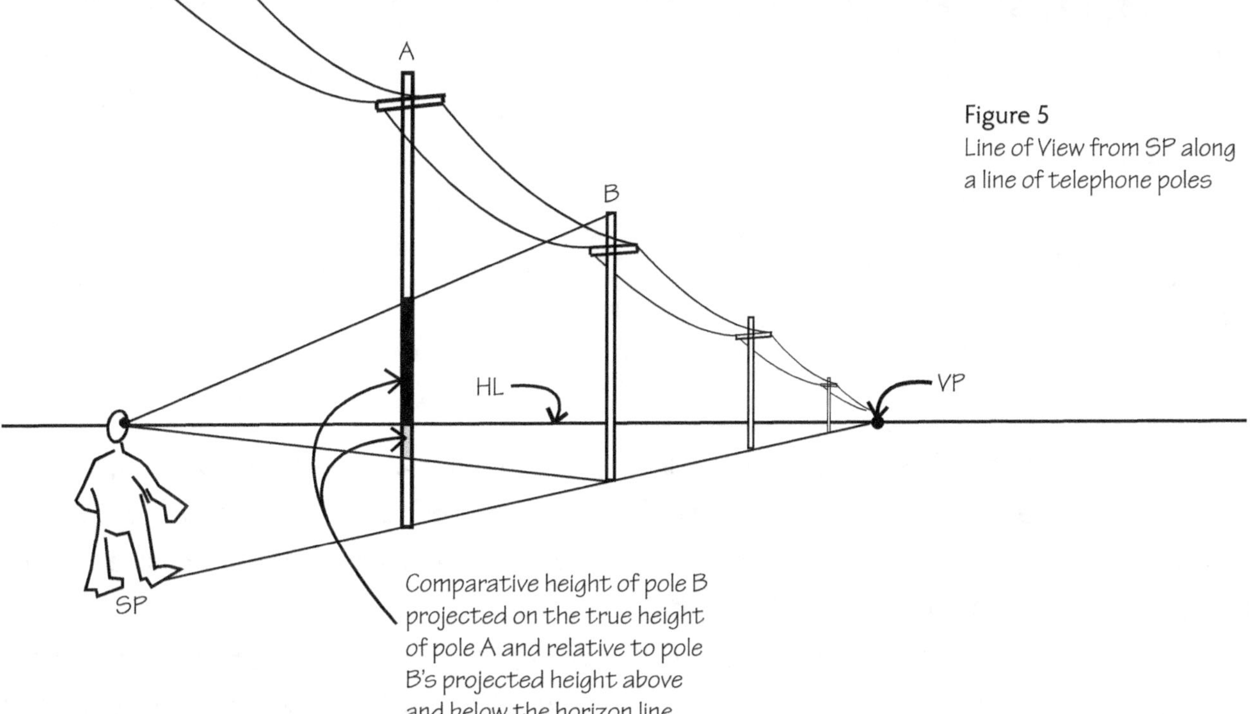

Figure 5
Line of View from SP along
a line of telephone poles

Comparative height of pole B
projected on the true height
of pole A and relative to pole
B's projected height above
and below the horizon line

all other poles on the measured pole. You would now know the apparent heights of all the poles (corners in Figure 6) relative to the measured pole (true height line).

If we could rotate corners B & D of our object directly behind corner A, as shown in Figure 6, we could look through Corner A and note the apparent height of corners B & D relative to the height of Corner A.

Corner A (in Figure 6), is the only part of our object touching the Picture Plane and will become our True Height Line (THL) and the line on which all images of the vertical heights of all other corners will be recorded.

Corner A also represents a vertical section through the Picture Plane and becomes an important element in our final perspective drawing.

We can now quickly construct a Vertical Diagram of the situation as simulated in Figure 6. The Ground Plane, Horizon Line, and Station Point are located, and corners A, B, and D are simulated as vertical lines A-A', B-B', and D-D' and are placed on the diagram relative to their distances from the Station Point. (These distances can be transferred directly from Figure 6 to the Vertical Diagram by the use of dividers)

Figure 6
Line of View from SP through
corner A to corners B & D

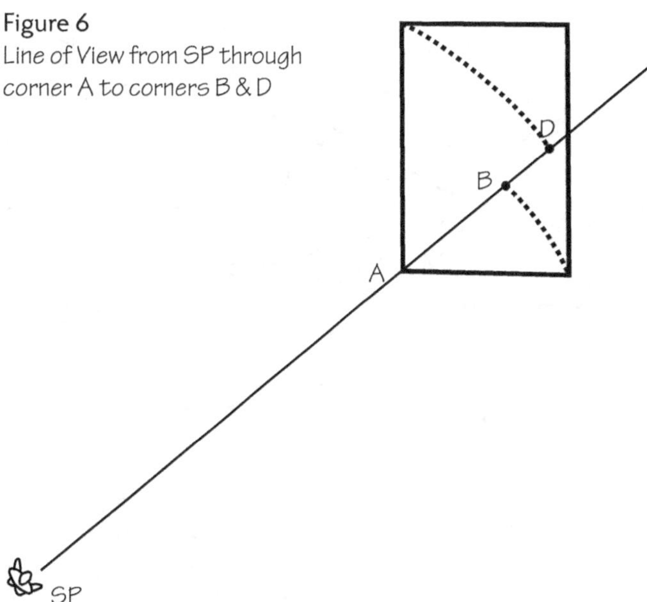

Remember, line A-A' is not only the True Height Line but is also a section through the Picture Plane. It is now simple to view the top and bottom of lines (or corners) B-B' and D-D' through A-A', and note on line A-A' where these points appear vertically on the section through the Picture Plane. You will remember that you have already located, on the Plan of the Picture Plane, points App, Bpp, and Dpp in the Plan as drawn in Figure 4.

These points can now be transferred to the Elevation of the Picture Plane (Figure 8).

The final drawing of the perspective can now be completed. In reality this perspective is a drawing of the Elevation of the Picture Plane.

At this point in the procedure, you can choose any scale for the final drawing that is convenient to the format of your drawing. In the adjacent example, Figure 8, a scale of twice the scale used to construct the Plan (Figure 4) and the Vertical Diagram (Figure 7) is being used.

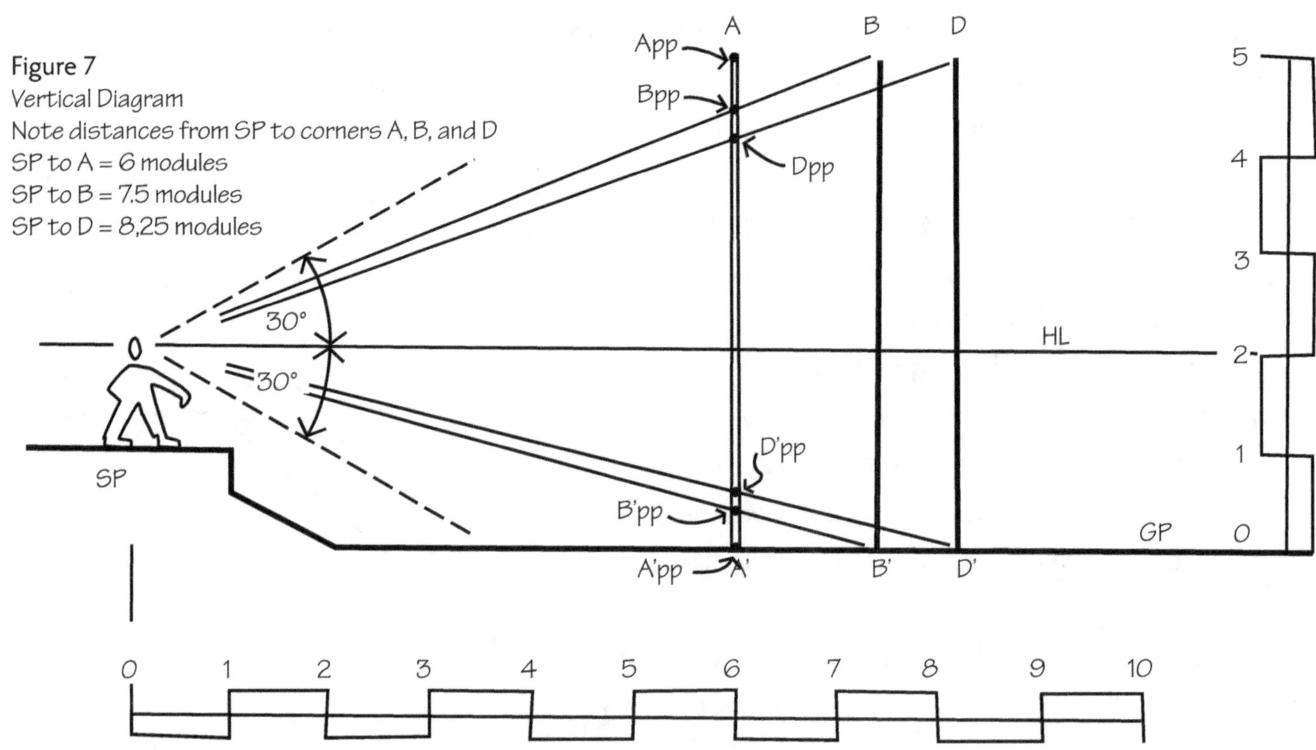

Figure 7
Vertical Diagram
Note distances from SP to corners A, B, and D
SP to A = 6 modules
SP to B = 7.5 modules
SP to D = 8,25 modules

28

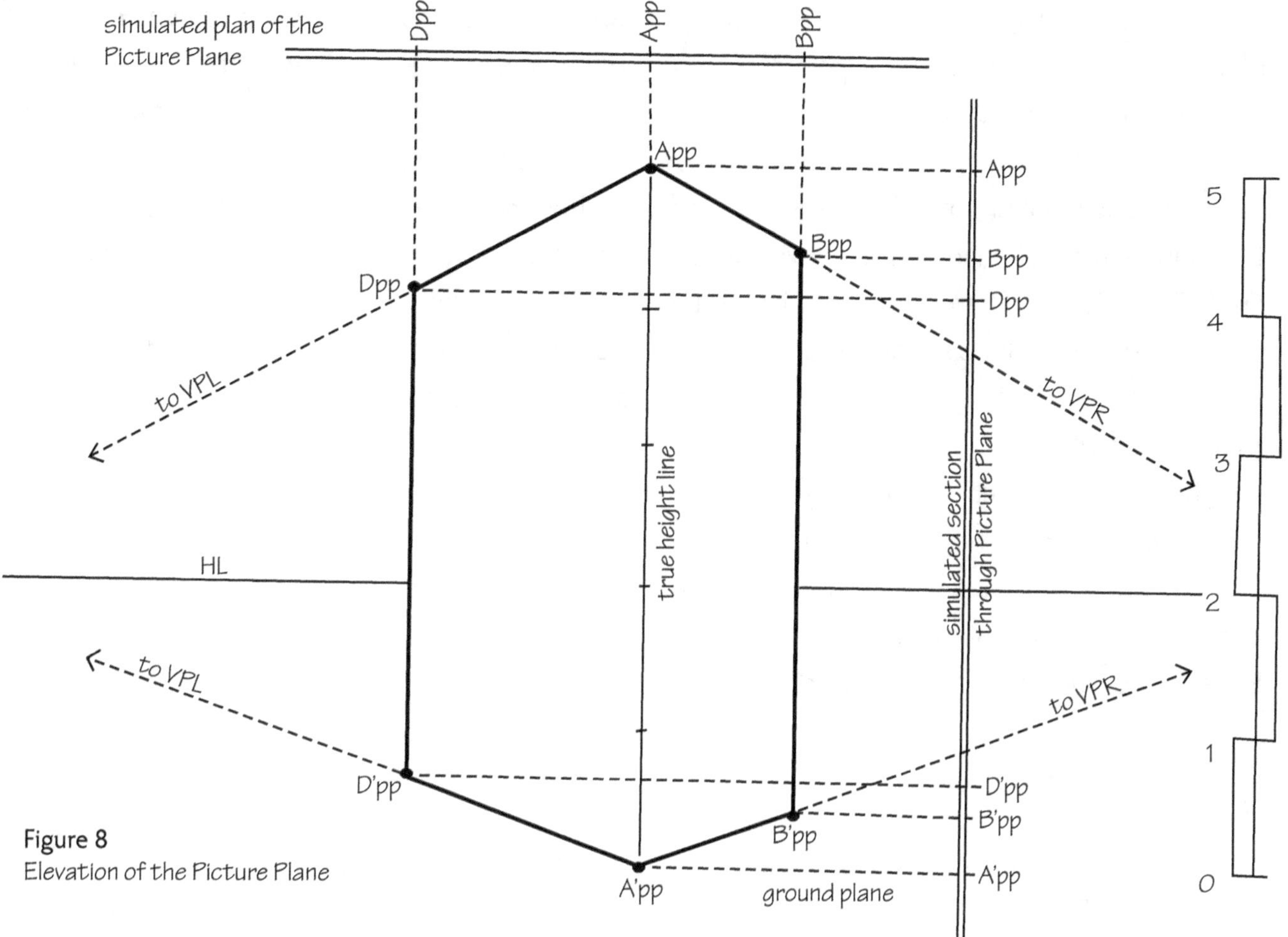

Figure 8
Elevation of the Picture Plane

In the upper margin of the drawing, draw a plan of the simulated Picture Plane transferred from the Plane generated in Figure 4 (remember you must double the scale if you want your final drawing doubled over the diagram).

In the right-hand margin of the drawing, simulate the section through the Picture Plane (double the scale as drawn in the Vertical Diagram, Figure 7).

The Horizon Line can now be located on the drawing.

Next, drop a line from point App on the simulated Plan of the Picture Plane to coincide with a line drawn horizontally from point App on the simulated section of the Picture Plane, to locate point App on the Elevation of the Picture Plane. In a like manner, find points A'pp, Bpp, B'pp, Dpp, and D'pp by dropping the plan of the Picture Plane to coincide with lines drawn horizontally from the Section through the Picture Plane.

It is now a simple matter to draw a line, on the Elevation of the Picture Plane, from App to Bpp and App to Dpp, to define the top of the object and a line from A'pp to B'pp and D'pp to define the bottom.

If it is important to the designer to locate the vanishing points, a line from App through Bpp to the Horizon Line will locate the VPR and a line from App through Dpp to the Horizon Line will locate the VPL.

Interpolation

If one chooses not to use physical vanishing points, or, if the vanishing points fall off the surface of the drawing board, the designer can interpolate a series of guide lines on the surface of the drawing.

In Figure 9 below, the mass of the building, which has been created by the Projected Image Method, has been divided into 4 equal segments by dividing each vertical line by 4 equally spaced points. A line drawn between each point then vanishes to its true vanishing point. The designer can then draw smaller elements in perspective by eye or by subdividing the larger sements into smaller segments. Of course, the designer can divide the vertical lines into as many segments as necessary relative to the scale of the mass to be interpolated.

Figure 9
Interpolation Diagram

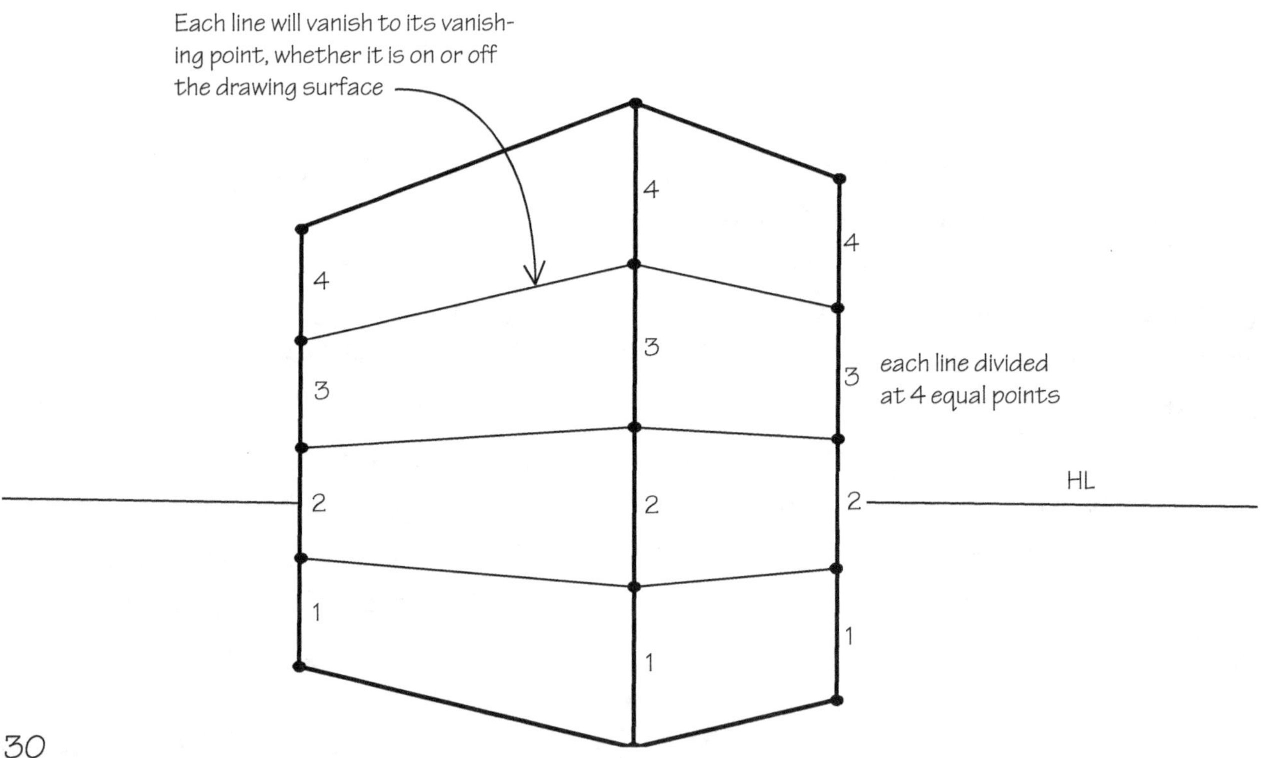

The Projected Image perspective system can also be helpful in creating, in perspective, a modular framework or "wire cage" through which the designer can organize space and form during the design process. In my opinion, the modular frame is a much better method of perspective construction than the perspective charts in use today as these charts force the designer into a choice of station point location that may or may not be the best choice of the position from which the object should be viewed.

Begin by selecting a basic cube of a size that works best with the scale of the design decisions to be made. One might choose a five-foot cube for the analysis of functions of small scale or a cube of ten or twenty feet on each side for projects of larger scale or projects of urban scale.

The designer must choose the relationship of the viewer (SP) to the Ground Plane and the angle from which he or she wishes to view the Base Cube. The limits of the growth of the cube framework must also be predictable as any cubes growing vertically or horizontally out of the vertical or horizontal cone of vision will quickly be distorted.

To construct the modular framework, draw the Plan of the base cube, locate the Station Point and the ℄ of the horizontal cone of vision, and draw the Picture Plane 90° to this ℄. Draw lines from corners A, B, and D of the cube to the Station Point and note where these lines cross the Picture Plane (see Figure 10).

Measure the distances from the SP to corners A, B, and D, and construct the Vertical Diagram. Locate the horizon line and choose the distance from the horizon line to the Ground Plane.

Transfer the simulated plan of the Picture Plane (Figure 10) and the Simulated Section through the Picture Plane (Figure 11) to the Elevation Of The Picture Plane (see Figure 12 on the next page).

Draw the Base Cube on the Elevation Of The Picture Plane as in Figure 8 and, if convenient, locate vanishing points VPL & VPR.

The Base Cube can now be expanded vertically by the use of the True Height Line and the VPL and VPR.

One of the major principles of perspective is that any set of lines parallel to each other will vanish to the same point. Using this principle, draw a line from corner A' on the Base Cube through corner D to intersect with a line drawn in a similar manner on the cube above the Base Cube. This will create VP-1. In a like manner, draw a line from A' on the Base Cube through B to a point of intersection with a line drawn in a similar manner on the cube above the Base Cube. This will create VP-2.

By using the VPL and the VPR and VP-1 and VP-2, the construction of the modular framework can now be completed.

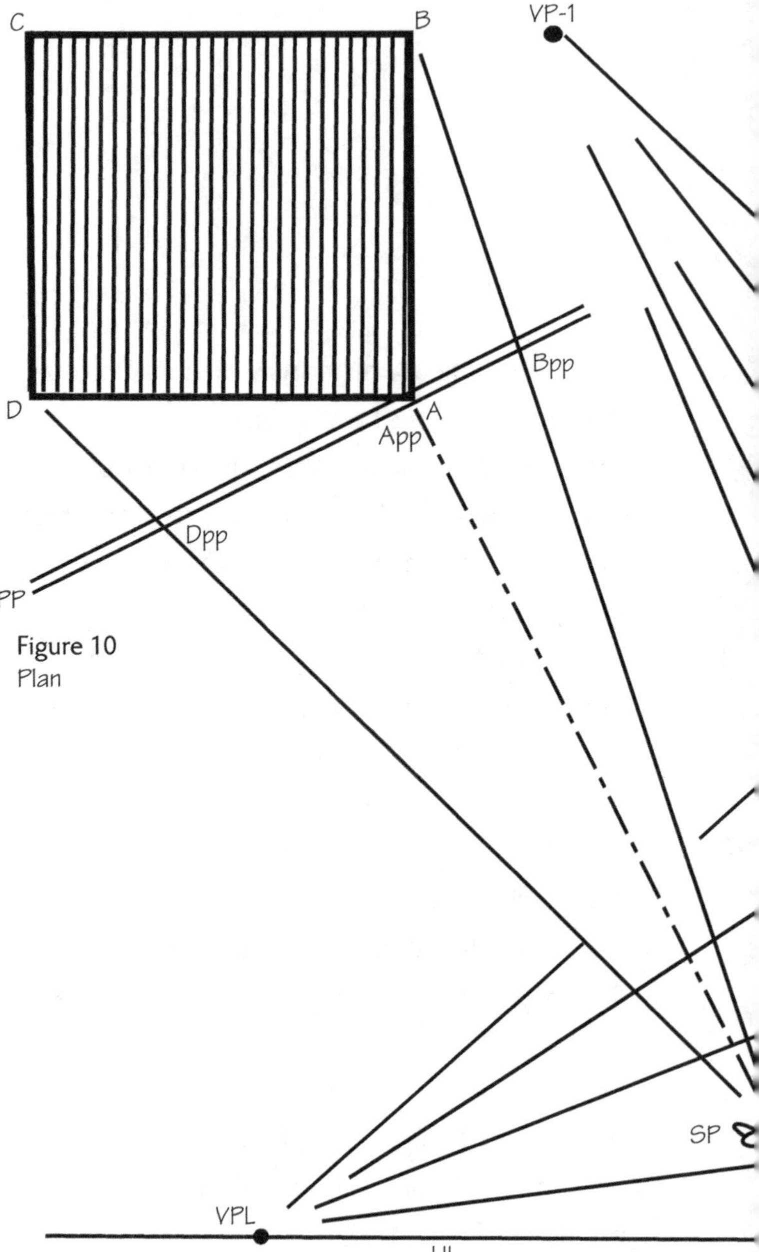

Figure 10
Plan

Figure 11
Vertical Diagram

Figure 12
Elevation of the Picture Plane

VP-2

simulated plan of
Picture Plane

Dpp
App
Bpp

true height line

simulated section
through Picture Plane

App
Dpp
Bpp

SP

D

B

VPR

A'

A'pp

App   A
Bpp
Dpp

B

D

A'pp

A'

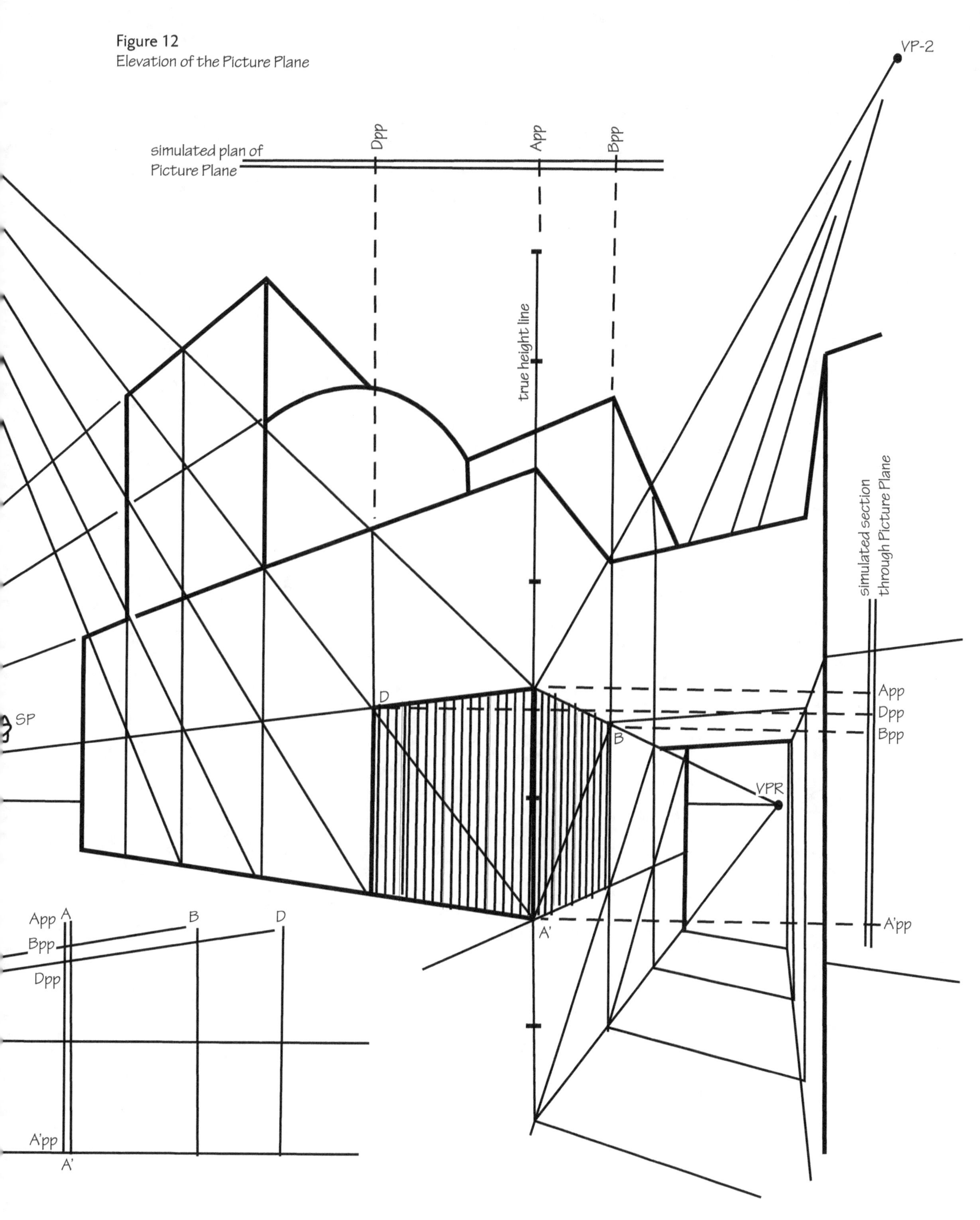

Chapter 3

The One-Point Perspective

The one-point perspective is quite easy to construct and is a quick and easy way to examine interior and small exterior spaces; however, large interior spaces and most exterior spaces are best analyzed by the use of the two- or three-point perspective. The one-point perspective, if not used appropriately, tends to create a static interpretation of space and form.

The basic definition of a one-point perspective is that the centerline of the horizontal cone of vision is perpendicular or parallel to most planes in the object being drawn, and the centerline of the vertical cone of vision is on the horizon line.

All perspective drawing requires an understanding of the cone of vision of the human eyes, as this cone of vision will dictate what the viewer is—and is not—able to see, and thus able to draw without distortion.

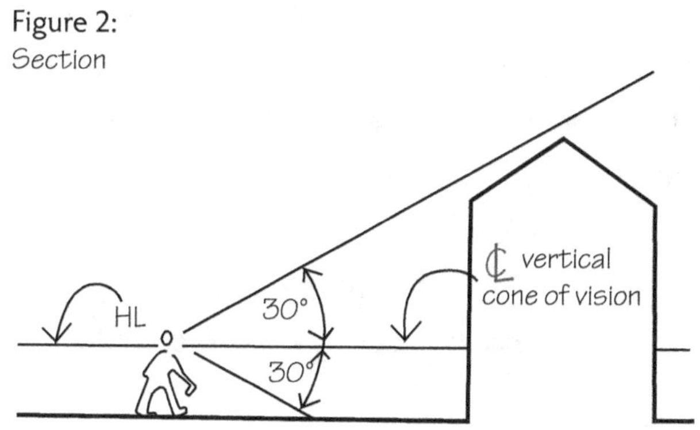

The horizontal and vertical cone of vision, for the one-point perspective is illustrated in Figure 1 and Figure 2.

The Plan drawing, in Figure 1, shows the centerline of the horizontal cone of vision located at the center of the building. This is, of course, not necessary as the centerline of the horizontal cone of vision can be placed anywhere on the building or space that best explains the designer's intention. In Figure 3 below, the centerline of the horizontal cone of vision has been moved off center of the object to be drawn.

You can see that this movement off center has caused the viewer (station point) to move further from the object being drawn, as the corner of the building to the right of the viewer could not be included in the drawing if the viewer were to move closer. Movement off center is not to be discouraged as spaces many times are best explained off the main axis of a particular space or building.

The following examples will show the entire procedure leading to the completion of a one-point perspective. An interior space will be used in our case study, as small interior spaces are best suited to the one-point interpretation.

Remember, the one-point perspective is constrained by the limitations of the centerline of the horizontal cone of vision being fixed at 90° to, or parallel to, the planes to be drawn, and the centerline of the vertical cone of vision must be on the horizon line.

Step 1: Lay out the plan of the situation, locate the position of the viewer, (station point) and, within the limitations of the cone of vision, what portion of the space being viewed will be included in your drawing. (see Figure 4)

You will notice the inclusion of the Picture Plane in Figure 4. The Picture Plane is exactly what the name implies; it is a plane that the viewer looks through and on which an image of objects beyond (and sometimes in front of) appear. Think of the Picture Plane as a large sheet of glass, placed vertically at the point of intersection of your cone of vision and the object or space being drawn. The Picture Plane is not unlike the film in your camera on which an image of what you see is

Figure 3
Plan

captured in the photograph. In a one-point perspective the Vanishing Point becomes an automatic resultant of the centerline of the viewer's horizontal and vertical cone of vision.

All lines, parallel to the centerline of the horizontal cone of vision, will vanish to this point. All other lines will be horizontal or vertical.

Figure 4
Plan

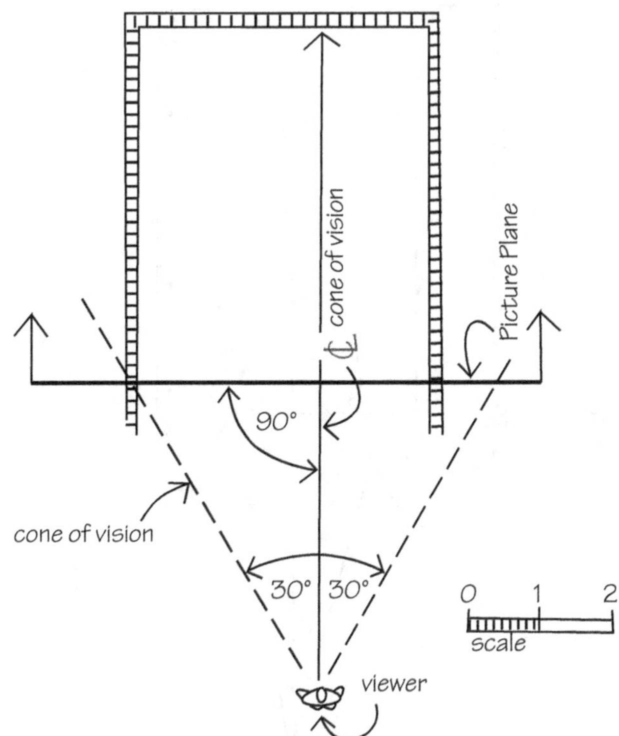

Step 2: Make a vertical section of the situation. It will be convenient to make this section at the Picture Plane. In other words, this section actually becomes an elevation of the Picture Plane. The location of the Horizon Line and the Vanishing Point will be established in this drawing (Figure 5).

You will notice that Figure 5 is entitled "Elevation Of Picture Plane" as this is exactly what it is. Everything that touches this plane is True Height and True Width, and all objects falling behind this plane will be measured relative to this plane.

Figure 5
Elevation of Picture Plane

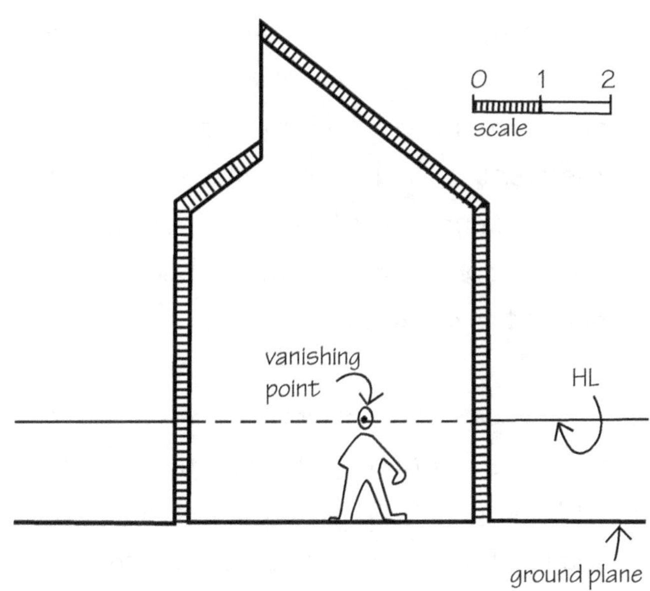

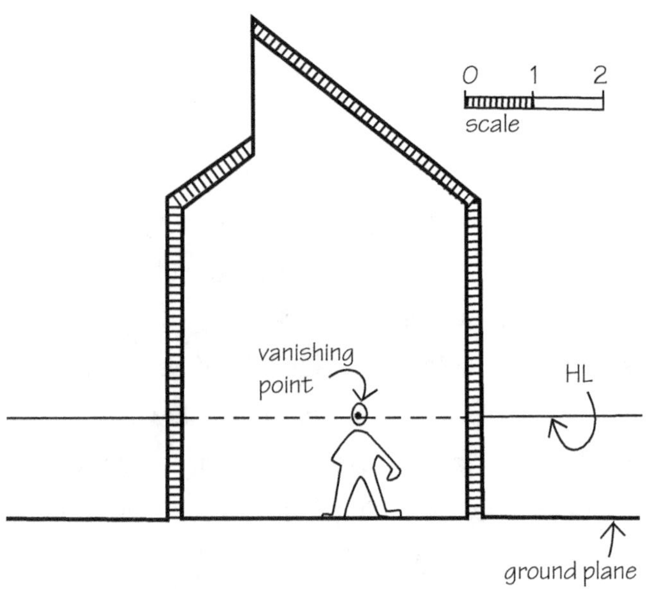

You will also notice that the Vanishing Point has been located (see Figure 5 above, repeated here for ease of reference). Remember, in a one-point perspective, the vanishing point is always on the horizon line and always at the vertical and horizontal centerline of the viewer's cone of vision.

Because of the speed with which the one-point perspective can be set up and constructed, it is valuable to examine your space from several different station points. The great value in the examination of architectural space and form in perspective is to allow a confident flow of spatial decisions during the development of your design.

Step 3: In Figure 6, lines are drawn from the Station Point to corners B and C, and the points at which these lines cross the Picture Plane are noted. It is convenient

to divide the Picture Plane into modules to easily locate these points of crossing, or to change scale between the Plan drawing (Figure 6) and the Elevation Of The Picture Plane, (Figure 7). You can also use a set of dividers to measure from the ℄ of the cone of vision to points C', E', and B'. You can double or triple these dimensions from the plan diagram depending on the desired size of the final perspective drawing.

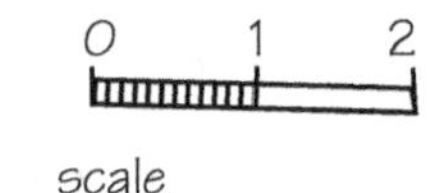

note: The Picture Plane in figure 6 has been divided into modules of measurement. In Figure 7 (to the right), the scale has been doubled.

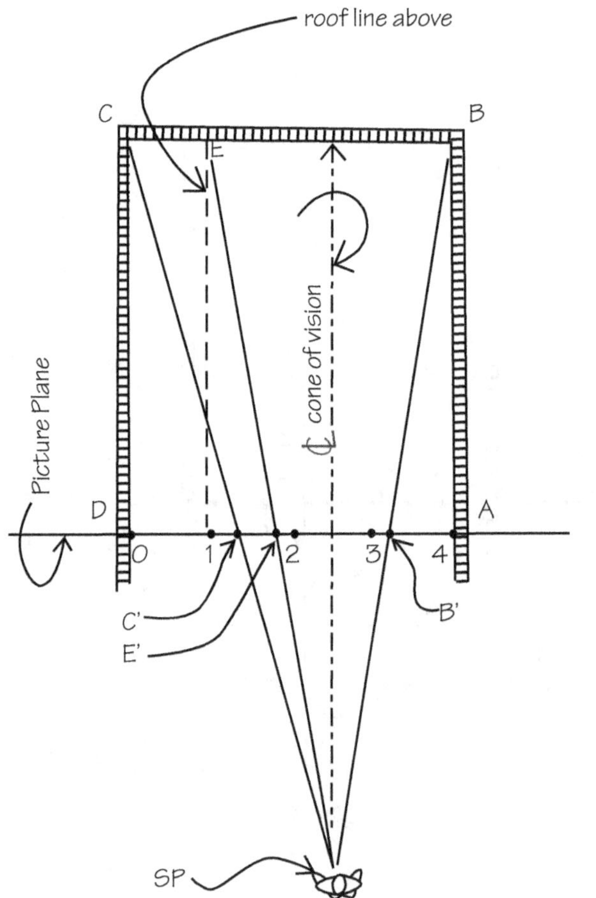

You can see from figure 6 that a line drawn from the station point to corner B crosses the Picture Plane ± 3/4 modules left of corner A, and a line drawn from the station point to corner C, crosses the Picture Plane ± 1 1/3 modules to the right of corner D. These points can now be transferred to the Elevation Of The Picure Plane, figure 7, and are noted as shown.

Step 4: It is now convenient to draw all lines that are parallel to the centerline of the cone of vision to the vanishing point (as in Figure 7). You can now extend point B (the image of corner B' on the Picture Plane) vertically to intersect with the line drawn from corner A to the Vanishing Point. The intersection of these two lines becomes corner B in perspective. In a like manner, corner C can be found by extending the point C' vertically to intersect with the line from D to the vanishing point. This intersection becomes corner C. It's now all a matter of transferring lines and finding intersections.

figure 7
Elevation of the Picture Plane

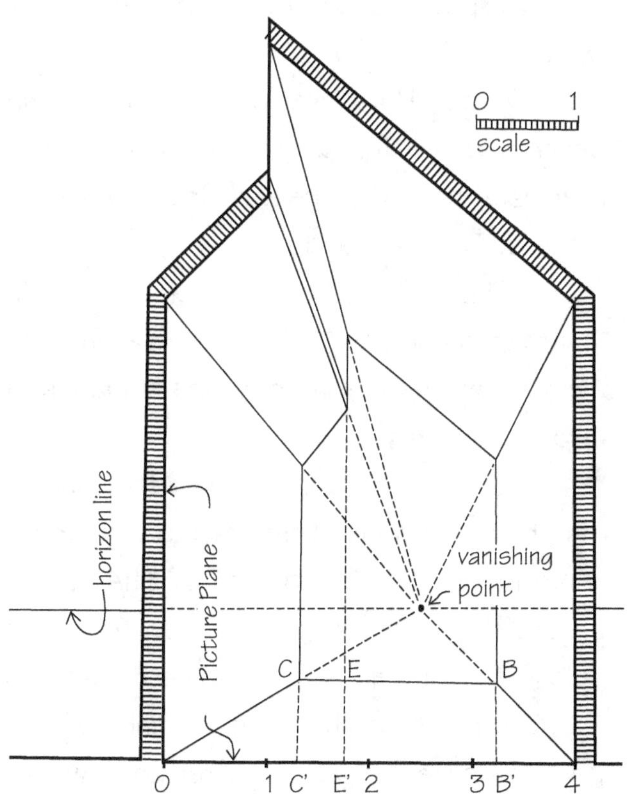

By connecting corners C and B, and by extending lines vertically from corners C and B to an intersection with the lines previously drawn in perspective from the Picture Plane, the rear plane of the space will be created.

All subsequent elements within the space are located in the same manner as described above, except that objects that are freestanding within the space can best be located as described in Step 5, as follows.

Step 5: Location of Objects Within the Space.

Objects that are located within the space are easily found by the same basic principle used to locate the wall, floor, and ceiling planes in Figures 6 and 7.

In Figure 8, a plan similar to the plan in Figure 6 is shown. Added to this plan is an element of one-by-one modules in plan, and two modules high.

One method to locate the freestanding object (and probably the best method) is to locate the "footprint" of the object on the floor plane of the space. To locate this footprint, first extend lines from the Station Point to the front corners of the object, corners F and G, and note where

these lines fall on the Picture Plane, namely points F' and G'. These points will locate the side-to-side limits of the front of the object's footprint.

Next, draw lines HJ and GK to one side of the space from the object to be located.

Figure 8
Plan

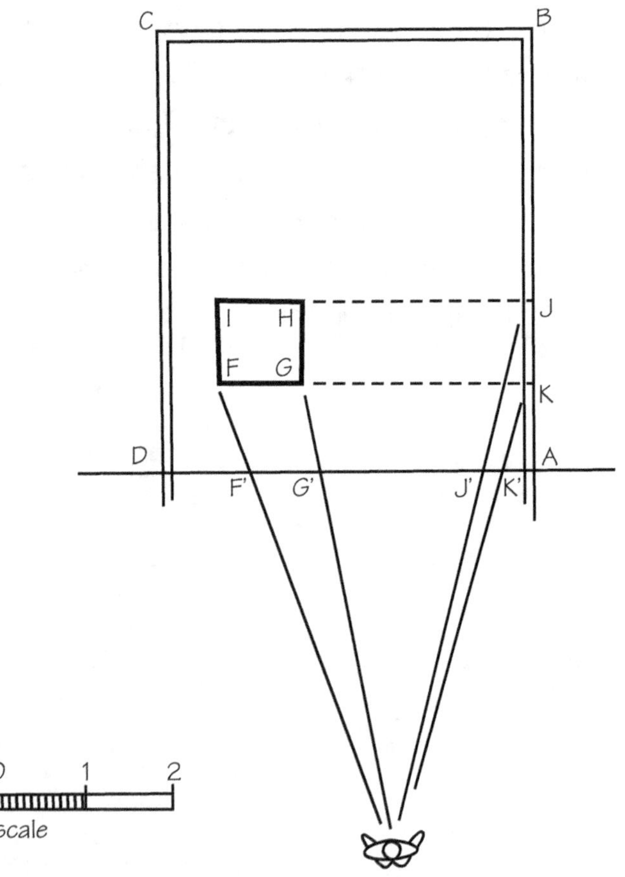

40

Draw lines from the Station Point to points J and K and note where the image of these points fall on the Picture Plane (points J' and K'). This will establish the front and rear limits of the object's footprint.

Next, as shown in Figure 9, extend point K' vertically to meet line A-B. This point of intersection is the front limit of the object's footprint. Likewise extend J' vertically to line A-B to find the object's rear limit.

Extend points F' and G' vertically to meet a line drawn horizontally from the front limit of the object's footprint. The intersection of these lines is the front line of the object's footprint. The rear limits of the footprint can be found in a similar manner.

To locate the object's height, draw a line from a two-module height (of the object) on the Picture Plane to the Vanishing Point. Extend points J' and K' vertically to a point of intersection with this two-module-high line.

The horizontal extension of these points of intersection with a vertical extension of points F' and G' will locate the top of our object.

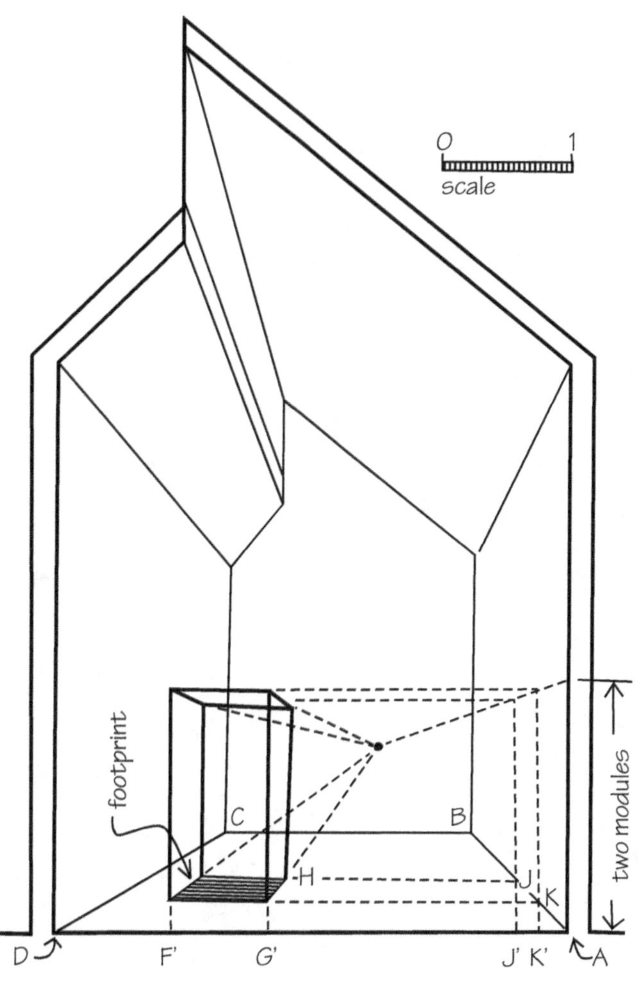

Figure 9
Elevation of the Picture Plane

CHAPTER 4

The Three-Point Perspective

When viewing very high interior or exterior spaces or objects from high above or below, the three-point perspective is the most appropriate drawing. The main advantage of the three-point drawing is that it allows the viewer (SP) to move much closer into the space or closer to the object being viewed than allowed by the one- or two-point perspective drawing (see Figure 3, Chapter 1 on page 14).

Because the ℄ of the viewer's vertical cone of vision must be on the horizon line, the one- and two-point perspectives move the viewer back from the space or object. Many times this condition moves the viewer completely out of the space and therefore a drawing depicting the space accurately is impossible.

The three-point drawing allows the viewer (SP) to cast the 60° vertical cone of vision upward or downward without being constrained by the horizon line being on the ℄ of the vertical cone of vision.

The three-point perspective has been historically avoided by designers because of the laborious methods that have been required to construct the three-point drawing using conventional methods. Using the Projected Image system, the three-point drawing is quite easy to construct.

The system of constructing the three-point perspective is similar to the system used in the construction of the two-point perspective, the only difference being that the picture plane in the Vertical Diagram (see Figure 4 on page 46) will not be perpendicular to the horizon line and ground plane.

Because the picture plane is always perpendicular to the ℄ of the cone of vision, the picture plane will never be vertical in a three-point perspective (see Figure 13, Chapter 1 on page 19).

To begin the construction of a three-point perspective, the designer must first determine the relationship of the viewer's position (SP) to the object to be drawn. This relationship must be established both horizontally and vertically. In the three-point perspective, it is usually the vertical cone of vision that controls the distance from the viewer to the object, as normally a three-point perspective is only used when the object or space is higher than it is wide.

In the example in Figure 1, you can see that the object to be drawn is five modules high and we are viewing the object nine modules above the ground plane (GP). As we cast our vertical cone of vision downward from the horizon line (HL), you can see that the base of the object can be no closer than five modules horizontally from the viewer. If the viewer were to move closer to the object, the cone of vision would be violated and the bottom of the object would become distorted in the drawing.

After determining how far the viewer (SP) must be away from the nearest corner of the object, the designer must now choose the view he or she wishes to have of the face and sides of the object, and at what point on the object he or she wishes to locate the ℄ of the horizontal cone of vision (℄ HCV). The horizontal location of the station point

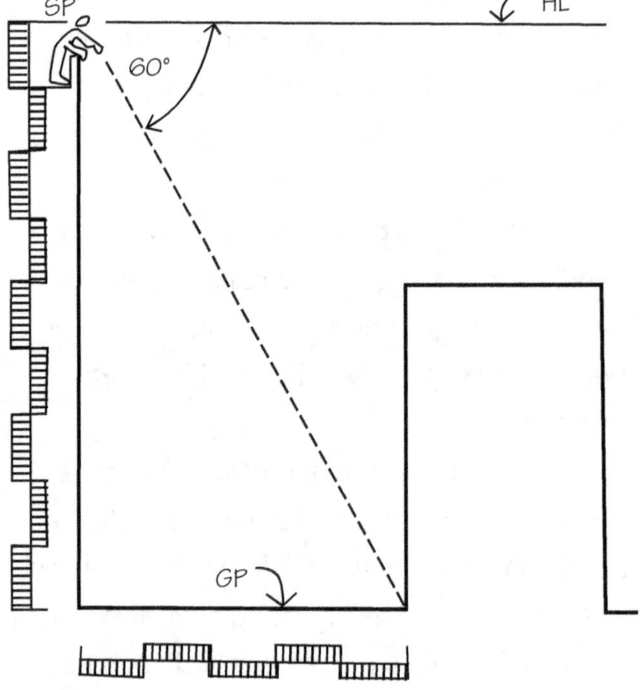

Figure 1
Vertical Location of the SP

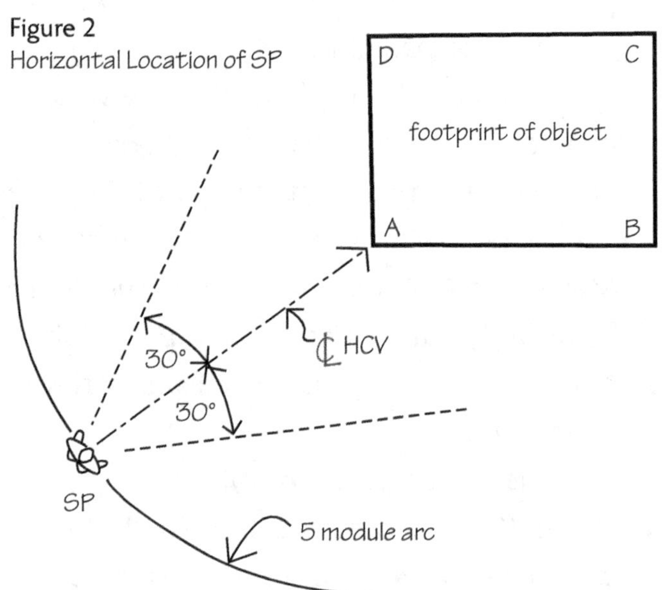

(Figure 2) was controlled by the five-module constraint placed on this location by the vertical cone of vision (Figure 1). The location of the SP below could have been at any point on the five module arc desired by the designer as long as this location does not violate the designer's 60° horizontal cone of vision.

At this point in the Projected Image process, it is convenient to measure the distances from the SP to corners A, B, and D of the object. These distances will be needed to draw the Vertical Diagram, which is the next step in the construction of our three-point perspective (see Figure 3 below).

Figure 3
Distances of object's
corners from the SP

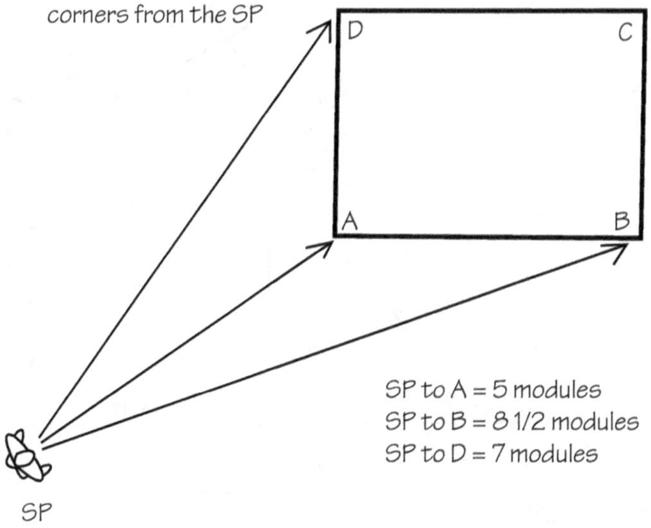

SP to A = 5 modules
SP to B = 8 1/2 modules
SP to D = 7 modules

The Vertical Diagram

Using the location of the station point as determined both vertically and horizontally in Figure 1 and Figure 2, we can now construct the Vertical Diagram. As you will recall in the two-point perspective, discussed in Chapter 2, the Vertical Diagram was constructed to simulate the distance that each major corner was located away from the station point. The same basic diagram is also applicable to the three-point perspective drawing.

As shown in Figure 4, make a diagram of the location of corners A, B, and D relative to the station point. This is done in the exact way that the Vertical Diagram was constructed in Chapter 2, Figure 8 (page 28). Next, locate the ₵ of the vertical cone of vision and create the Picture Plane 90° to this ₵ . Pass this Picture Plane through the top of corner A. This will create a Picture Plane that is a diagonal line running from the horizon line to the ground plane. This diagonal Picture Plane is the only difference between the Vertical Diagrams for the two- and three-point perspective drawing.

We can now draw lines from the station point (SP) to the top and bottom of each of the simulated corners in the Vertical Diagram (Figure 5)

Figure 4
Vertical Diagram

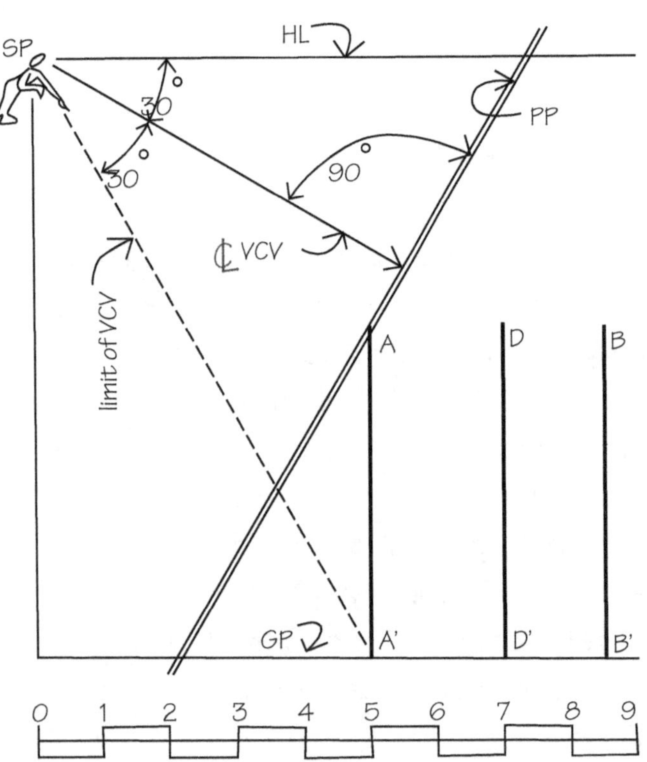

Figure 5
Vertical Diagram

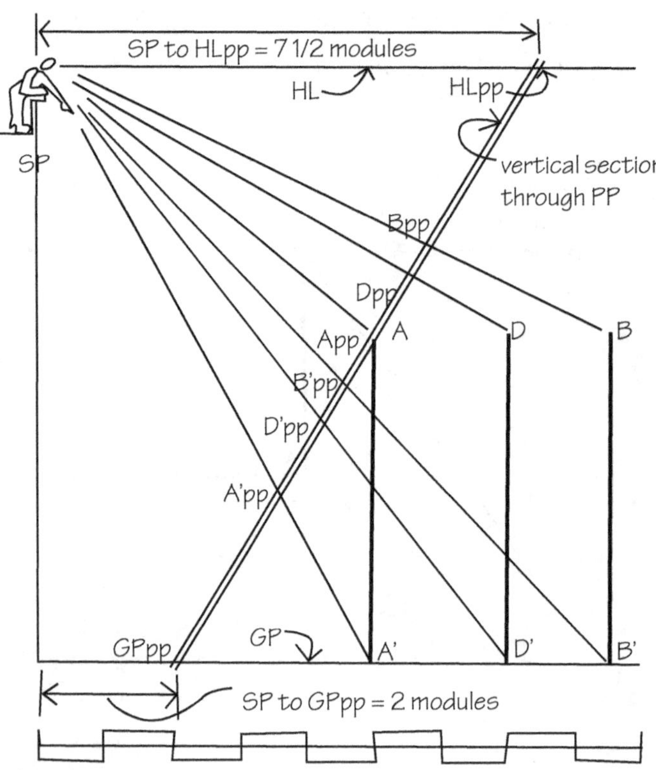

and note where the images of these points fall on the Picture Plane.

Lines drawn from the SP to the top of corners A, B, and D create points App, Bpp, and Dpp, and lines drawn from the SP to the bottom of corners A, B, and D create points A'pp, B'pp, and D'pp (You will remember from chapter 2 that the notation "pp" denotes that this point is the image of a point on the picture plane as seen from the station point).

You will notice in Figure 5 that the Picture Plane cuts through the horizon line at point HLpp and through the ground plane at point GPpp. As the distances from the station point to the corners—in the Vertical Diagram—assist us in the location of the vanishing points in the Projected Image system, the distance from the Station Point to the HLpp and GPpp will be crucial in the location of the third vanishing point. This vertical picture plane will be transferred to our final drawing to locate all vertical points.

The Plan or Horizontal Diagram can now be completed (Figure 6). Using the horizontal location of the station point, as determined in Figure 2, draw the ℄ of the horizontal cone of vision to the same corner (corner A) that

the vertical picture plane has been passed through (see Figure 4). This corner will also become the only vertical line in the drawing and will be the line from which all future vertical measurements will be taken.

The next step is unique to the Projected Image system in that two horizontal (plan) sections through the picture plane will be diagrammed: one where the picture plane intersects the horizon line and one where the

Figure 6
Plan-Horizontal Diagram

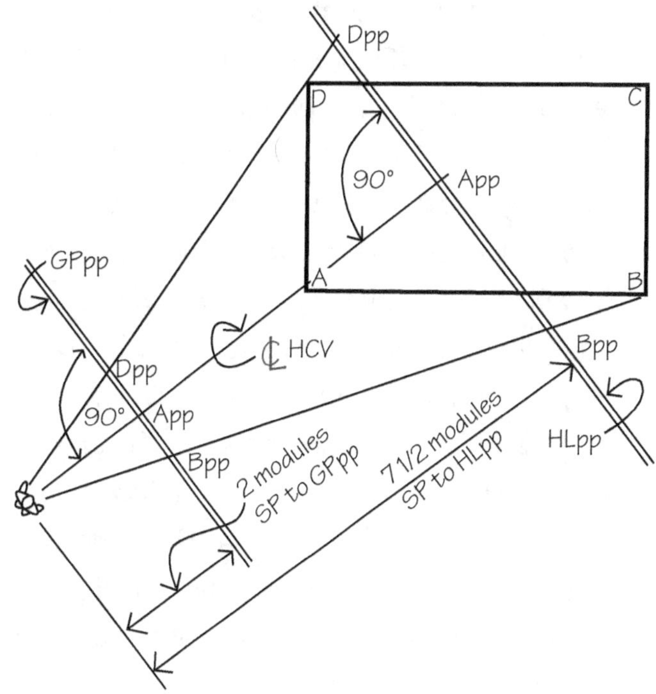

picture plane intersects the ground plane (see Figure 5, showing the distance from the SP to HLpp = 7 ½ modules, and the distance from the SP to GPpp = 2 modules).

In the Plan or Horizontal Diagram (see Figure 6) locate the two plan sections through the picture plane 90° to the ₵ HCV. (Remember, SP to HLpp is 7 ½ modules and SP to GPpp is 2 modules.)

By drawing lines from the SP through corners A, B, and D, points App, Bpp, and Dpp will be located on the picture plane at HLpp, and on the picture plane at GPpp.

The final perspective drawing can now be completed (see Figures 7 and 8 as intermediate steps to the final perspective in Figure 9 on page 50). Remember that a perspective drawing is really a drawing of the elevation of the picture plane. The image of our building on the plan of the picture plane at the horizon line (HLpp) can now be simulated by line Dpp-App-Bpp and the image of our building on the plan of the picture plane at the ground plane (GPpp) can also be simulated by line Dpp-App-Bpp. (Obviously line Dpp-App-Bpp appears shorter on GPpp than on HLpp as GPpp is much closer to the station point than HLpp; see Figure 5)

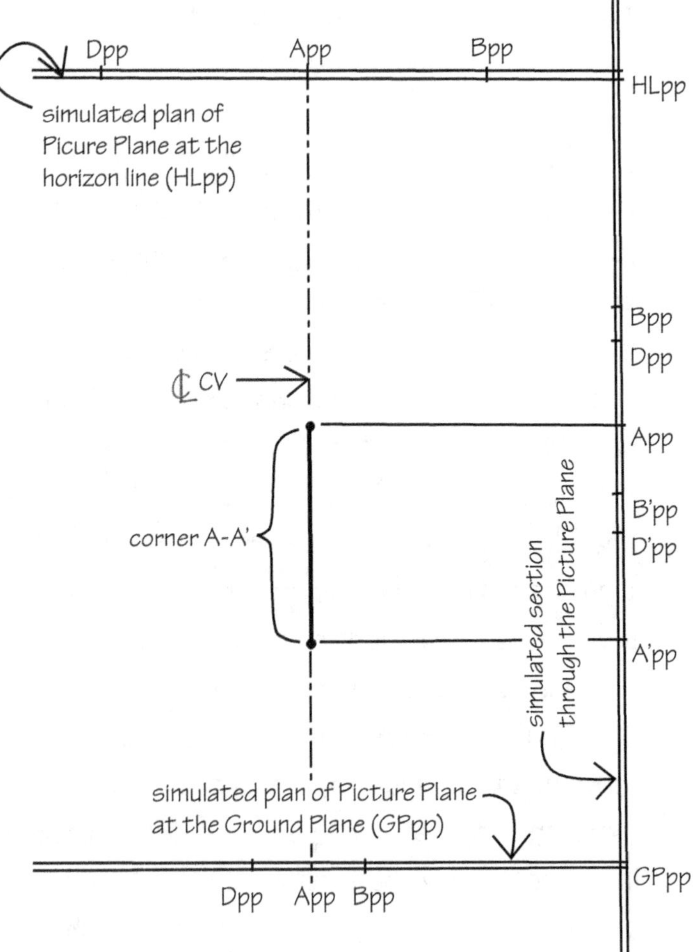

Figure 7
Elevation of the Picture Plane

48

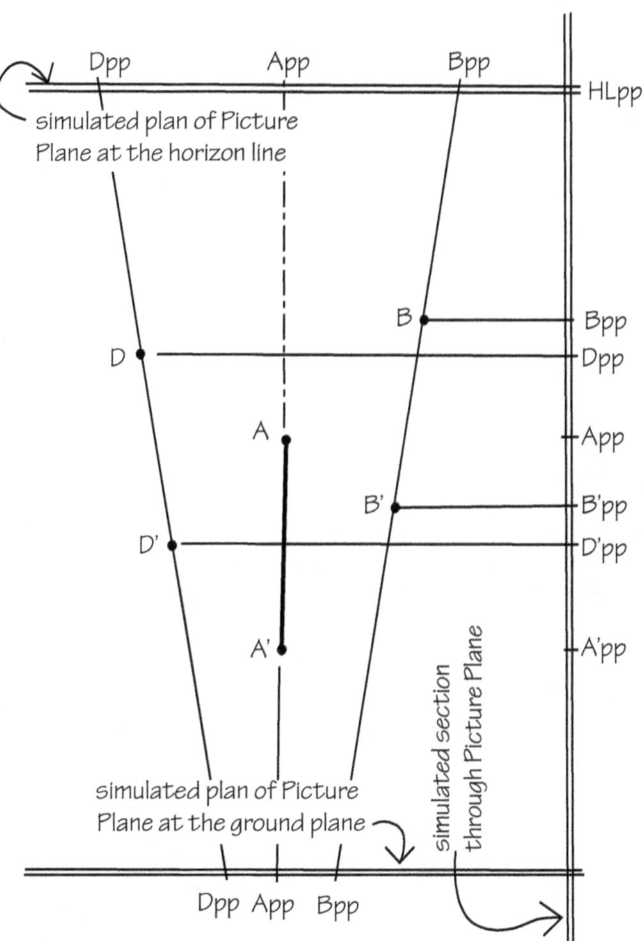

In the right-hand margin of the Elevation of the Picture Plane, simulate the vertical section through the Picture Plane as generated in the Vertical Diagram (Figure 5).

Lines can now be drawn horizontally from points App and A'pp, on the simulated section through the picture plane, to intersect with the ₵CV. This will create corner A-A' and will become the line from which all vertical measurements will be taken.

Lines can now be drawn from Dpp and HLpp to Dpp at GPpp to create the vertical edge of corner D-D', and from Bpp at HLpp to Bpp at GPpp to create the vertical edge of corner B-B'. It is now a simple matter to find the top and bottom of corners B-B' and corner D-D' by extending lines horizontally from the simulated section through the picture plane to points on these vertical edge lines. For example, a line extended from point Dpp, on the simulated section through the picture plane, to a line from Dpp on the horizon line (HLpp) to Dpp on the ground plane (GPpp), will create point D on the Elevation of the Picture Plane. Point D is the top of corner D-D'.

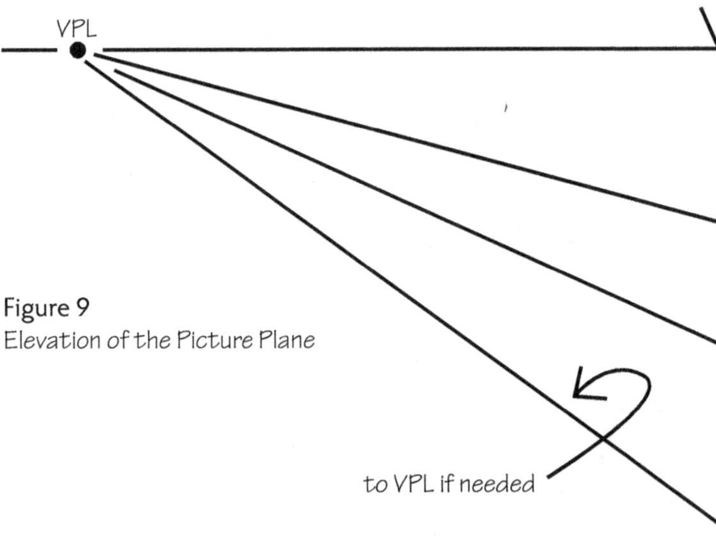

Figure 9
Elevation of the Picture Plane

In a like manner, points B and B' can be located creating the top and bottom of corner B-B'.

A line can now be drawn from point A to point D to create the top left edge of our building and if the line from A is extended through point D to the horizon line, the vanishing point to the left (VPL) will be established. In a like manner, a line drawn from point A to point B to create the top right edge of our building, if extended through B to the horizon line, will create the vanishing point to the right (VPR).

A line drawn from D to D' will create corner D-D' and, if extended to meet the ℄ of the cone of vision (℄CV) will create the third vanishing point (VP3).

It is now a simple matter to complete our perspective. Even though the creation of the vanishing points has been shown in Figure 9, vanishing points are unnecessary when using the Projected Image system, as all elements of the drawing can be located without the use of vanishing points if such points are inconvenient.

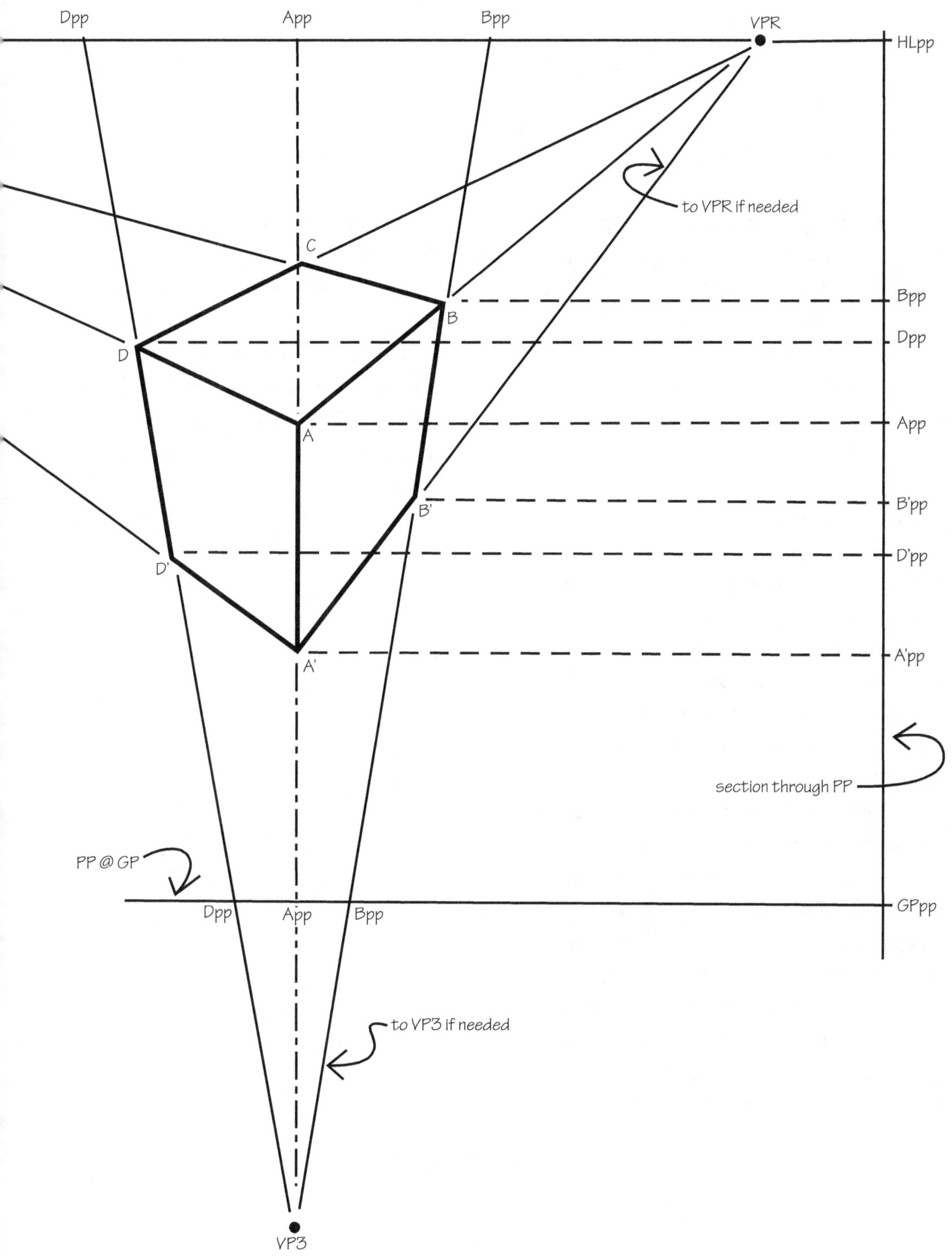

Dpp
App
Bpp
VPR
HLpp
to VPR if needed
C
Bpp
B
Dpp
D
App
A
B'pp
B'
D'pp
D'
A'pp
A'
section through PP
PP @ GP
Dpp
App
Bpp
GPpp
to VP3 if needed
VP3

In the foregoing discussion of the three-point perspective using the Projected Image system, the horizontal vanishing points were created by the relative heights of the corners. The vertical vanishing point (VP3) was created after diagramming the image of the picture plane at the horizon line and at the ground plane.

There are two purposes for such a detailed discussion of the rationale behind this vanishing point location effort. One, it is most important that a designer understands the theory behind any exercise, and two, many times one of the horizontal vanishing points falls off the drawing surface and cannot be conveniently reached. This is also true of the vertical, or third, vanishing point.

Most importantly, the designer must be able to orchestrate the station point location relative to the spatial concept of his or her design, and should never fall victim to the "magic" of any perspective method that he or she does not thoroughly understand.

However, after understanding the concept of the Projected Image system, there are a few shortcuts to the location of the horizontal and vertical vanishing points, if there is space on the drawing surface for the location of such points.

It is a well-known principle of perspective drawing that all sets of parallel lines vanish to the same point and the VPL and VPR can be found by drawing lines from the station point at 90° to each other and parallel to the major planes of the object being drawn (see Figure 10). Where these lines intersect with the picture plane at HLpp can be noted and placed on the simulated plan of the picture plane. These points then become VPL and VPR.

Using the same principle of parallel lines vanishing to the same point, the third vanishing point can be quickly located on the section through the Picture Plane by extending the picture plane to intersect with a line drawn vertically downward from the station point (see Figure 11). The intersection of these two lines is the third vanishing point and can be transferred directly to the final drawing.

Figure 10
Plan (Horizontal Diagram)

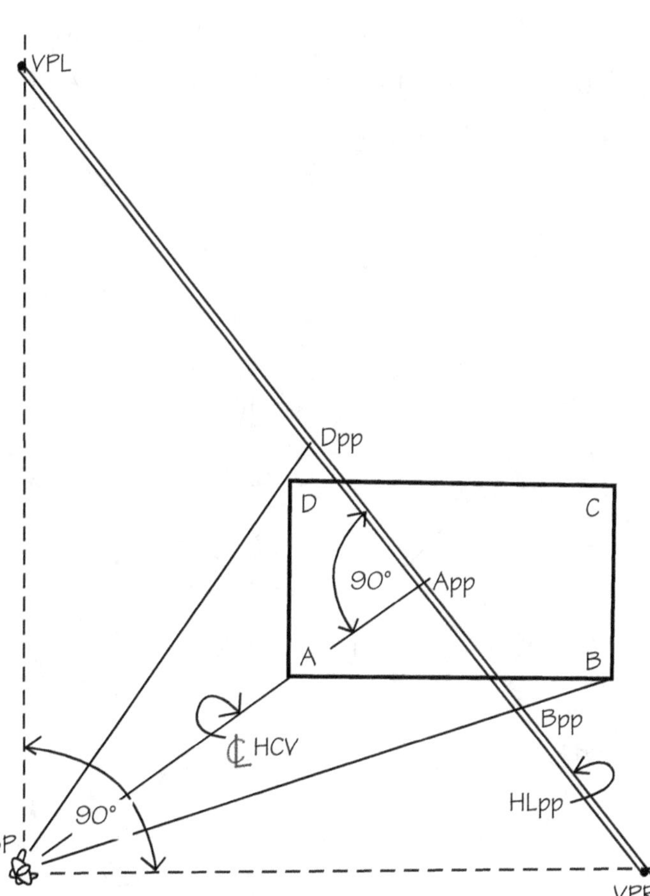

Figure 11
Vertical Diagram

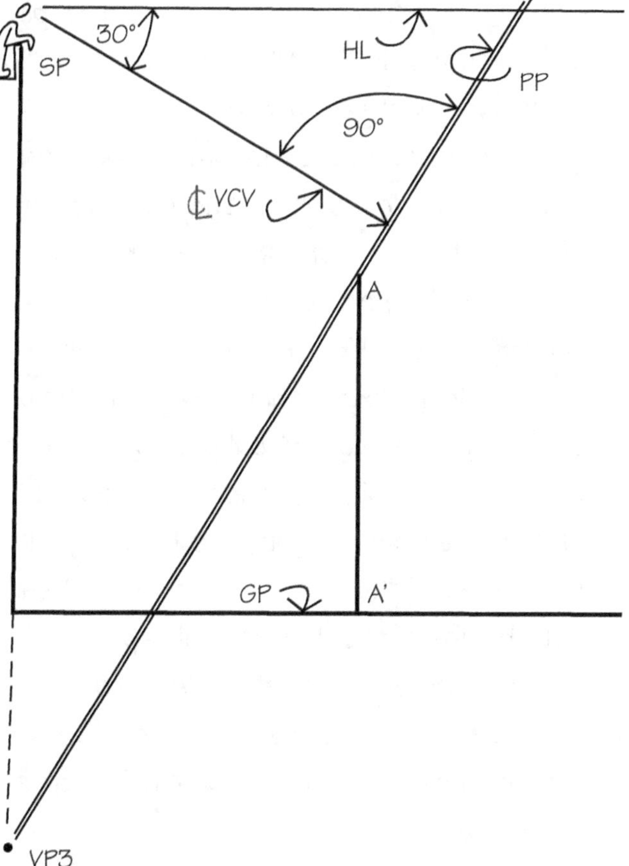

Dealing with the "Far" Vanishing Point

In a two-point perspective drawing, especially in a perspective where the angle of the centerline of the horizontal cone of vision ($\mathcal{C}$HCV) is nearly perpendicular or parallel to the major planes of the space, one of the vanishing points (VP) usually falls off the drawing surface. Conversely, the other vanishing point normal falls well on the drawing surface. It is therefore difficult, if not impossible, to use this "far" VP in the construction of the perspective drawing.

There is a constant relationship between the location of the station point (SP) and the two horizontal vanishing points in a two-point perspective. In other words, if the SP and one VP is known, the other VP is automatically fixed. Therefore, with the use of one VP and the vertical projection of the corners of the object, as located on the plan of the Picture Plane (PP)(see Figure 1), all of the planes of the object can be located without the use of the "far" vanishing point.

The following steps will lead to a quick resolution of a two-point perspective without the need to locate or use the far vanishing point.

Step 1: Draw the Plan, locate the SP, draw the PP 90° to the $\mathcal{C}$HCV and establish points App, Bpp, Cpp, and Dpp on the Picture Plane (Figure 12).

Step 2: Establish VPRpp, the "near" VP on the Plan of the PP by extending a line from the SP parallel to line AD to the PP (Figure 12).

Step 3: Extend line BC to the PP and establish point BCpp. This will establish a second True Height Line (THL), which has been noted as Bpp-B'pp in fig. 13. Line App-A'pp (in Figure 13) is also a THL as corner A of our object falls on the PP.

Figure 12
Plan

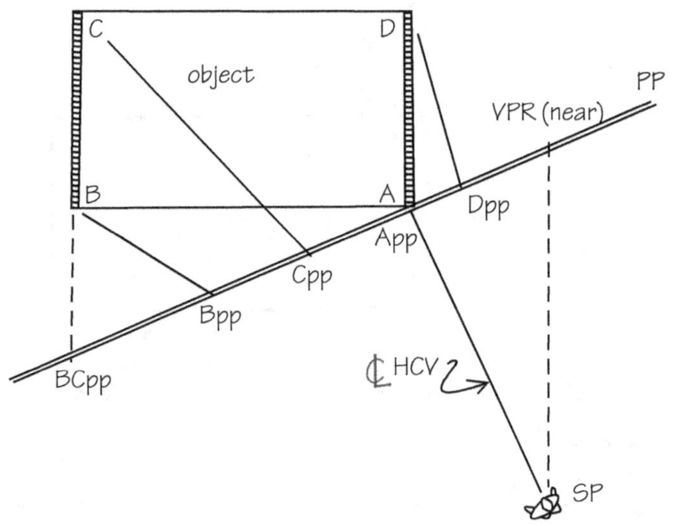

Step 4: Draw the Elevation of the Picture Plane (Figure 13), locate the horizon line (HL) and corner A-A', the true height line (THL). In the example in Figure 13, the HL has been set at one module above the GP, and the height of the object has been set at four modules.

Step 5: Draw the ground line (GL) on the Elevation of the Picture Plane, and transfer points BCpp, Bpp, Cpp, App, Dpp, and VPRpp from the plan of the PP to the GL.

Step 6: Locate the VPR (near) on the horizon line (HL) and draw lines from points App and A'pp to the VPR.

Step 7: Draw a line vertically from point BCpp four modules high above the GL. This will establish THL#2, which would be an image of corner B-B', if corner B-B' was projected forward, in perspective, to the PP.

Step 8: Draw a line from the top and bottom of THL#2 to VPR. This will establish plane Bpp-B'pp-VPR, on which plane B'-B, C'-C will be located.

Step 9: It is now a simple matter to extend lines upward from the GP from points Bpp, Cpp, App, and Dpp to create all of the planes needed to complete the perspective without the use of the "far" vanishing point (VPL).

Figure 13
Elevation of the Picture Plane

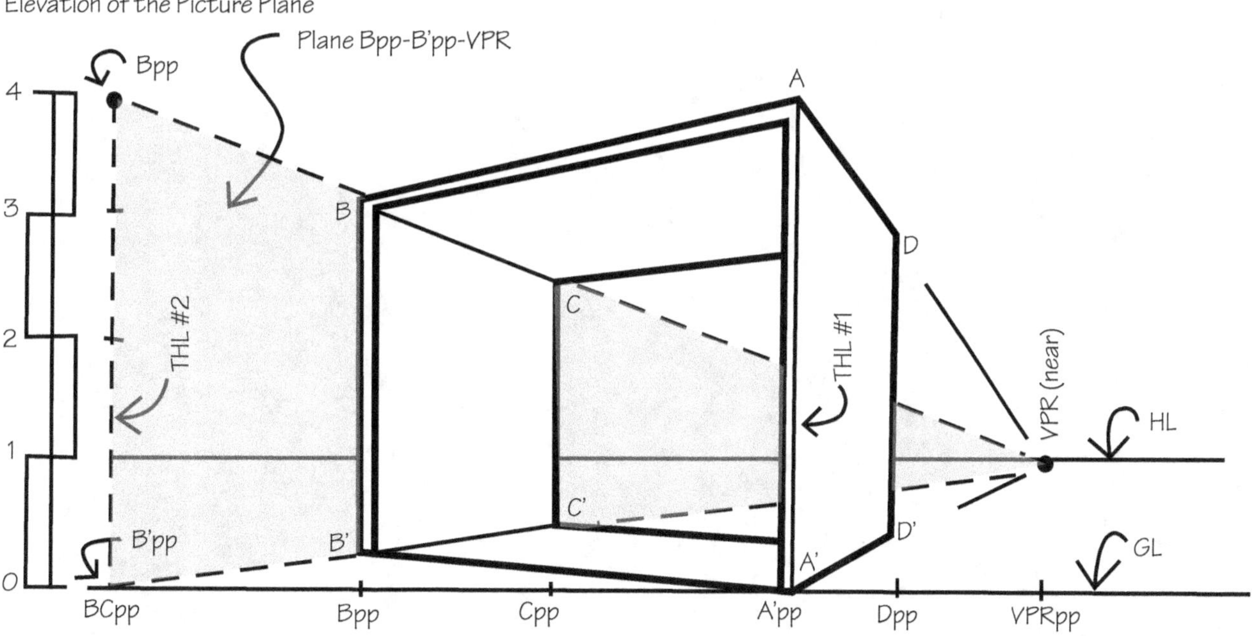

CHAPTER 5

Conclusion

The drawing of a quick and accurate perspective is an important design tool. You will grow exponentially as a designer with the ability to spatially examine your design as you participate in the design process. I believe that the basic genesis of architectural form is space. Many design with the belief that form creates space; I disagree. I believe that space creates form. Designers who seek exterior form and impart this form on the interior spaces deny the functions, both physical and metaphysical, that should be the innards of the form. As I continually remind my design students, one should not be surprised by the shape of a banana after it has been peeled. A banana is beautiful because, when peeled, the fruit (the real function) is revealed as the generator of the peel, the outward form. The peel does not generate the banana.

It is easy to make a floor plan that the designer thinks resolves the functional needs of the client and the wrap such a design in an outer skin created to aesthetically please the client and the general public. These designers are cosmetologists that try to hide the inner faults with a false facade. If these designers had made an exterior form that honestly mirrored the interior arrangements of their design they would be dismayed with the misshaped pile that they had created. All the architects that I know who design in plan and elevation and only use the perspective as a presentation medium or a "selling point" miss the true understanding of "architecture as space."

Do not misunderstand me. Creating a form that is an expression of interior spaces and the resultant structure and materials is an extremely difficult effort; consuming many more hours than making a floor plan and applying a cosmetic facade. An honest effort at form giving not only springs from the scale of the inner spaces, but also from the need to make peace with the surrounding neighborhood, be it man-made or natural. To bring all these physical and metaphysical forces to rest is more difficult and is the constant agony and joy of the honest designer. Real art or the attempt to create art is what makes me understand why Vincent Van Gogh cut off his ear. Those architects that are cosmetic form givers have an easy task during their so-called design process. As far as I know all their ears are intact.

Being able to draw a quick and accurate perspective of the spatial sequences within your design is only important if you can't do it. Do not become mesmerized with your ability to make beautiful drawings. Accurate drawing of architectural space is a language; no more, no less. A language you must master if you are going to be able to speak to yourself, much less to others. More important is the nurturing of your design philosophy and the wisdom of your design concepts; these are the elements that will be the measure of your contribution to society. But language is important. Language is not in itself an idea but is the medium by which we communicate ideas to others. A perspective is no more than a two-dimensional drawing of a three-dimensional object or space. A perspective is only an illusion, but a very important architectural language.